31·3

TO LIVE IT IS TO KNOW IT

TO LIVE IT IS TO KNOW IT

From Jamaica to Yorkshire –
the life story of Alfred Williams

ALFRED WILLIAMS

and

RAY BROWN

NP

NORMAL PRODUCTIONS
2003

Published by
NORMAL PRODUCTIONS
The Redhouse
30 Spencer Place
Leeds LS7 4BR.

First published by Yorkshire Arts Circus 1987

Printed in Great Britain by Peepal Tree Press
Leeds.

ISBN 0-9544997-0-0

Life is good and life is Hell and it the same life.
Sometime you choose how you see it.
Sometime there is no choice.

ALFRED WILLIAMS
1918 - 1997

INTRODUCTIONS TO FIRST EDITION

Reason I writing this book now is I everlasting looking back at nineteen twenty five, remembering things that happen, what life like as I progress through. When I think of this book, I know just what must go in. Maybe things from my life some use to younger people. It not a lot I can do, I an ordinary man, but what I know, I did not learn in books, I did learn from living it!

And this book, I do not think it my book! I just tell what I know, and I tell it for my son who born here in England. I would like him to know what Hell older ones were meeting. One day my son, and all other kids, might be really stuck in bad times. I want my son to know where he from so that he can remember, and say, 'My family, they meet it hard, I can put up fight against this, it nothing near what they went through.'

I only tell truth in this book, truth as it in my memory. I do not remember exact day or exact distance between two places. But I remember what happen and I tell what happen.

When I think of my life I think I been sucking salt through wooden spoon. Try to understand what that like: when you five year old somebody give you salt jar, put wooden spoon in, other end of spoon go in your mouth. Then they say, 'Start sucking!' Now I nearly seventy and I been sucking that salt every day of my life. Plenty people will say, 'That funny! That a joke!' Let them try. Take salt and spoon and start to suck, then you know what my life feel like…

Alfred Williams, Leeds, 1987.

Alfred Williams is my friend and neighbour. For the last few years we have exchanged views on many topics. In the summer of 1986 we began this book together. We have talked and tape recorded, read and re-read, drafted and redrafted.

Neither one of us could have written the book without the other. Our friendship has been strengthened by this collaboration.

After a long session, when Alfred had taken me back into his childhood, he laughed and said, 'I give you the broken language, the funny talk, now you suck salt! Knit fog!' It has been a privilege to work with someone who knows so much. I hope people will read Alfred's book and understand some of the lessons he paid so dearly to learn.

Ray Brown, Leeds, 1987.

INTRODUCTION TO SECOND EDITION.

In 1981 I bought a Victorian house from an eccentric. To put it politely, the house was full of junk. The stone terrace, built 1854, had suffered urban blight. When the proposed road failed to materialise, Victoria Terrace became a Housing Action Area. Walk the unpaved back road as it was when I moved in with my new partner Ros, my two kids and her one: no. 1 - empty; no. 2 - Frank Kelly, drop-out electronic genius; no. 3 - empty (although it housed a collapsed grand piano!); No. 4 - empty; no. 5 – Alfred Williams with his wife Monica and toddler Michael; no. 6 - Pat and Al social/community workers. And I bought the last in the row from the eccentric, Samual Palmer (It is still known as 'Sam's').

The first time I met Alfred we got off to a fine misunderstanding. I introduced myself as Ray. 'Hello, Mr Ray,' he said, 'My name is Williams.' I assumed the 'Mr' was banter and I didn't hear the 's' on Williams. So for a week or two he called me Mr Ray and I called him William. In fact, over the years, we often used the 'Mr' form as verbal daftness: 'Morning Mr Ray!', 'Morning Mr Williams!'

Everybody knew him as George, even Monica, his wife. It would be seven years before I knew his real name. By then we had become close friends and spent months writing this book.

It happened when the manuscript was finished, and to his great satisfaction, my partner Ros and I had read the whole thing to him, from beginning to end, in one sitting. "That's that then, Mr Willams!' I said. 'Only thing left is how you want your name: George Williams, G Williams or just Mr Williams… or is it Mr George Williams.' As I played around, in no doubt that his answer would be 'George Williams, you bogger,' his smile went. We sat at the big kitchen table in silence, then, to our astonishment, he said, 'Alfred Williams.'

Alfred, he explained, was his 'mother given name'. Years earlier he had worked at the Canada Dry soft drinks factory 'the first coloured there'. On arrival he was called George after Chicken George in ROOTS. The name stuck.

Would he like to go back to Alfred? Yes. Many of us began the process of replacing George by Alfred. It took time. We got there.

If we hadn't written this book, the change might never have happened.

Yorkshire Art Circus was a small community publisher, originally inspired by the dreams of social-ism, equality, and dignity for all. 'Everyone has a story to tell. We find ways of helping them tell it.' That was what would now be called their mission state-ment or vision (or have those formulations already been swept down the gutter of bureau-speak?).

My partner Ros and I had already worked on a YAC book. Trying to live as a writer I was sniffing around for another project. I was also gloriously involved in endless story swapping with, let's say 'George'. But no, I can't. It's too long ago. So – Alfred. Very few days went by without us laughing together about something or other. The source of our laughter could be painful or pleasurable.

I can't remember when the idea struck. 'Let's write your life story.'

Alfred's formal education was minimal. He had been an enthusiastic truant, 'I spent me school days up a tree!' he'd say, regret and delight in equal proportions. He never became a reader or writer and rarely attempted either. At first the thought of writing a book was alien to him. Gradually we worked out a way of doing it.

Once or twice a week we had a formal session: he would talk, I would sometimes ask a lot of questions, sometimes just listen, sometimes tape record the session. We always filled the kitchen with smoke from our pipes and his home grown tobacco.

Between sessions I drafted and redrafted, gradually shaping the material into sequences for the book, chopping and changing, adding material learned over our years of friendship.

It took a long time to find a written 'voice' that captured his voice and made it work on paper. Alfred's 'broken language' or 'funny talk' is, as you will discover, a rich mixture of Jamaican, Huddersfield, Leeds and tv-speak. I studied his grammar and it left me baffled. In the end I developed an intuitive understanding and found I could write 'Alfred' to Alfred's satisfaction.

When I had a few pages done to my satisfaction, I'd read them to Alfred. Then I made changes in the light of his reactions. In this way we put together the roughly twenty-odd thousand words of TO LIVE IT IS TO KNOW IT.

A great talker (yapping, he called it) Alfred had a fine sense of narrative rhythm and structure. He knew how he wanted the book to sound, when to insert a little humour, when to move and when to stop for a look round.

In the periods that I wrote, he was preparing for the next formal session. He sorted his memories. Not for Alfred the linear approach of the literate. It seemed to me that he arranged his memories like objects in a room... or a garden.

We had two disagreements during the writing of the book. Once he made me discard a whole chapter. 'It's wrong!' he said. I had written, from observation and memory, about his work in the Kirkstall allotments. 'If you want to know about cultivation, I tell you about cultivation.' My wrong chapter was replaced by the vivid sequence on rice growing.

The second disagreement concerned the lizard fights. When Alfred told me about catching lizards he was deeply distressed. I pulled out all the stops and wrote a piece that communicated this very clearly and also captured the sheer bloody cruelty of the fights. He decided he didn't want to share his pain and shame with others. On this one we compromised and included a rewrite.

The last chapter frightened me. We had on several occasions discussed religion, the Bible and creation myths. It seemed the right topic to end the book, it was a topic of increasing interest to him.

I was working on a green screen Amstrad, in the attic of Sam's. I read to him directly from the screen.

Trying to capture his views, I had decided to pack no punches. I presented his ruminations as I had heard them over the years. He sat in silence as I read from the screen. The sun sank and I didn't turn on the light. I finished. It was almost dark in the room, just the green glow illuminating us. I remember thinking I might have revealed a total misunderstanding of something fundamental to him. I might have blown the whole book. I might have lost one of the best friends I had ever had.

He greeted the end with silence and a long think. Then he pressed his hand on my leg and said. 'That right, man. That how I want to say it!' My relief and happiness were unlimited. I guess we went downstairs and opened a bottle, but I don't remember. I just remember the dwindling light, the silence as I read, the long slow think!

The book was published and well received.

Then we fell out for a while. The Guardian wanted to photograph him, Yorkshire TV wanted an interview. Alfred insisted that I tell both of them that he would comply for £2000. 'It doesn't work like that, Alfred,' I told him. 'Tell them to fuck off then,' he said. Alfred rarely used obscenities, but he was hurting. Some kind soul had told him that I had probably made thousands of pounds on the book. In fact the 7% royalties were equally split, we made a few hundred pounds each. He didn't think I had cheated him – but he did think I should have got us more money!

We fell out again during a late Eighties bout of local Labour Party sordid in-fighting. He was lead to believe that if he supported the Left he would lose his allotment! Also, just in passing, I was a criminal and the police had evidence! What upset me was that he wouldn't tell me who was doing the dirty work. He was afraid I would cause trouble and that it would come back on us both. Probably right on both counts.

Our friendship was strong, the estrangement lasted a few weeks. It upset us both a lot. We both left the Labour Party (or as I and thousands of others still like to say: the Labour Party left us).

We did many deliciously daft things together – driving to a sure-fire mushroom field at five in the morning, two buckets each, calling to each other across an expanse of dewy grass. We never found a mushroom. We laughed a lot. We usually did.

Once we went to Wales with Ros and our friend Andrew Lister. We hired a cottage in the Dovey Valley. It was drizzling when we arrived. We un-packed, picked rooms, then decided to walk up Cwm Cywarch. Alfred was mortified, why go out in the rain when we can sit and yap round the fire? We set out, leaving him to yap to himself. A few minutes after we passed the barking dogs, they barked again. We waited, suddenly there he was, dawdling after us in his battered trilby and donkey jacket. Later he agreed that it was a good idea, walking in the rain, it could be enjoyable. On the first night I made spaghetti. He never let me forget it, 'You say you is my friend, but you make me eat damned stringy stuff!'

In 1991 Ros and I left the Terrace and came to live in Chapeltown on the other side of Leeds. Alfred often rang, always introducing himself in the same way, 'Hello, brother.' We all missed the easy conversations in the kitchen. But we still did daft things. We were going on a North Sea fishing trip until Frank from No 2 asked if the boat would 'go out of our depth' and Alfred had the great idea of buying fish in Leeds market. The three of us did visit the Tropical House – where Alfred slid beneath the barrier, balanced on a stone in the artificial stream and pruned a banana plant. He must have been about seventy five at the time! He coloured his hair and had the actions of a sixty year old.

The Christmas before he died I was called to Leeds General Infirmary. The surgeon wanted to operate, Alfred refused consent until we had talked it through together. The surgeon gave him a few days to live, perhaps three or four months if he had the operation. I went with him as they wheeled him to the theatre. A doctor asked him when he was born – no answer. Again. No answer. A third time, close to his ear. Alfred whispered an answer. In the end he had to say it loud and clear – 'Nineteen eighteen'. Then he looked at me, his first smile of the encounter: 'Now you know, you bogger!'

Ros and I loved him and the feeling was mutual. We had no secrets from each other, and relied on each other's judgement in all major decisions. He was, I believe, a man of great wisdom and intelligence. Over the years I have come to the conclusion that, born into a white middle class environment, he would have ended up an academic philosopher or a captain of industry. Either way he would have been bigger than any narrow definition. Just as he was in his actual life.

When he fell ill Ros and I did what we could. We watched him die, he did so with great dignity and courage. I have appended two short pieces, written to commemorate him. He is unforgettable.

Ray Brown,
The Redhouse,
April 2003.

ONE

COMING THROUGH

Sometime there's a heel come down on the people of a country. The problems we had in the West Indies, I think they the same problems you get in this country. And what sort of problems you think they have in South American countries?

When I were young, in the West Indies, it were a bit different from here, but, as far as I know and realise, the heel that we people of Jamaica was under, English people was under it just the same. But I come to know this: every country have its rich and poor, its first class, second class and third class. Every country I know have the poverty stricken. But the poverty stricken here, in England now, they like the middle-class to the poverty stricken in Jamaica when I were a young boy.

That heel was on the neck as far back as I remember. Say I start about 1925, when I was a little boy. No use me writing about when I was born, you can't tell anyone about when you were born - you retain nothing. I don't know how things were in Jamaica at the time of my birth, but when I look back to when I was child, I see the pressure that was handed out to the West Indies... it was Hell. I don't know if is a book so long to tell the story of that pressure. Maybe it need everybody write a book.

Today kids are thinking it terrible hard over here, and things are getting tighter here, but, by God, it like Heaven to what I knew. Kids think it all flow for their parents like it flow for them. But when I young we get no help, no DHSS, no Welfare State, and labour exchange we had none.

So back in my young days, in Jamaica, the country is run by two men who were brothers, and they fight and argue like Margaret Thatcher and Neil Kinnock. But for all they say, they brothers. All this political fighting is just on the outside, they doing it to fool us; they just the same as each other - rich enough people. Middle class people. People wanting power and position. I don't write about these people, people who rule countries. I don't know about these people. And these people don't know about me.

I tell you first about the work I do as a kid, later I tell you about the school work I never do. I work for my father, and I work hard every day. Life wasn't Heaven for my father, he had horse, cow, goat, some field. But horses and such was cheap, and you didn't get a lot of money for them like you might now. So my father had some hard times, but he was a cruel man.

When I am about seven year old (which is when I started at school) I had to get up around five o'clock each morning and walk three mile to where my father pasture his horses for the night. I take the horses from the pasture and then I ride them to the common land, which is near my home. If he leave the horses on his pasture all the time, the feed there wouldn't be enough for them. Father also had pig, goat, and cow, and these animal require attention. I get home about eight o'clock and I get dress, tidy up and go to school - so my mother think.

I'm home again at twelve and ready for something to eat. School not far away, but I sometime going further than school. Afternoon school go on till four o'clock and I race home fast as I can. Time to catch the horses.

On the common land I find my father horses. Maybe two I catch, the others will follow. I'm only seven, but me alone I take the horses to the well, pull water. Round Mountainside, where I live, wells then were seven to twenty fathom deep. For a kid, pulling water from these well is hard work. I throw water in a trough and in this way water maybe five head of horse. Then I must take the horse the three mile back to my father pasture. And on way back home I collect the goats and bring them home with me; it not safe to leave goat out far from the house. And then I home, waiting for food and it's say half past six at night.

What hurts more than anything, that old man of mine, from the time I know I have a father, he never stretch out his hand with as much as a mint ball to give me as bit of encouragement. It still hurt me, all these year on.

I continue this work, with only the assistance and encouragement of my mother, until I am fourteen. About then I start to realise that the one or two pieces of clothes I have are wearing away fast. Mother did her best to keep them on my back, but father never show any concern.

At sixteen I'm left school and working the animals and the fields; each day I'm cultivating with my Dad. He make no changes. Nothing as encouragement, no extra clothing. It the same old story: no clothes except few I stand up and work in. Food I never short of, but money there is none.

And so, at sixteen, I look at myself and I say, 'What the hell must I do?'

I went to my mother, I could talk with her. I explain that my clothes wearing out fast, that I working all day in the field and with the horses, then going out on the street in the same few clothes and it show. Then I say, 'Look, it terrible, there is no betterment for me. I try to talk to him, I try to help, but I see no changes on the way.' Then I explain my intention, which is to leave. Mother did try to browbeat me, but I just tell her again that I'm leaving. The pressure was more than I could take.

Mother did not want me to go. I was her first child, a mother love her first more than second or third. Well, my mother did show to me that she always love me special like.

I went to live with my mother's sister, my Aunt Evelyn. Evelyn was glad to see me at first, I didn't know why. She live in Spanish Town and she have a dairy pen with a milk cow and calf, she supply milk to people.

Evelyn give me room to live and sleep in and she agree to pay me, to give me some wages for what I do for her.

So I start making attempt to get my head through, to find betterment. It was not a damned easy life. Where I am now, here in England, nobody really understand hardship I have known if they haven't been through it. Only to live it is to know it.

I get up in morning at four o'clock and I work all day till eight at night. With a cow you need to get her feed. You cut guinea grass each day. This grass is three, four foot high, like barley, say. It green, you bend low and cut it by the root, you make bundles of it and you carry it by the four or five bundles. These bundles you then put into a big chopping machine, and you turn the handle, turn the handle, and you just keep on turn the handle till all that guinea grass cut into short pieces. And it this chopped up grass you feed the cow. Without the chopped grass there no milk.

So for two years I work with Aunt Evelyn. Up at four and work until eight and all the time I'm getting my pay - fourteen shilling. Fourteen shilling not bad money, enough to buy pair of trouser and a shirt. But if you had to buy food, well, it could be ten shilling a week for food. To be truthful, Aunt Evelyn arrange to give me all my food and the fourteen shilling a week… when she is happy. When she is not happy, she doesn't give a damn.

After two year I look at myself and I say, 'What the hell I going to do?' I looked and I considered, and I decide that something better could be done.

I find work with a red face, a man you can call half-English, a so-call white man. I suspect this man father born English and come to live in West Indies. His name was Stafford Eunice and he come from

Kingston to take over his father farm when the father die. Eunice had near white skin and long, pretty hair. Good straight hair. English.

The so-call white in Jamaica, they are, what would you call them... they come from the slave drivers. Call them come-betweeners, they come between black and white in colour, nothing wrong with that. But they come between rich and poor, between white and black, handing out the pressure which white give to black when I a young man in Jamaica. The hardest time we had in our country was from the so-call white: descended from the slave driver and, when I started out making my way as a young man, still act like slave driver.

Eunice, he were so-call white, he was still a slave driver. A lot of these so-call whites like him, that is my experience. You can tell a difference between white and so-call white by the nose and the mouth. I get to realise for certain when I come to England and look at a lot of white faces. That was when I really learn the difference, but before that I could tell which was white and which was only so-call white.

I'm not trying to get myself on the white side, but when it come to my experience of the so-call white and the proper white, when I think of the so-call white, and how they treat me, I can't be drastic enough in what I say about them. This book only contain what I know, what I have experienced. When I remember them red-face come-betweeners, I some-time want to lash out at them. It is too late now and I could not do anything then. I could not tell them the truth then, but I can try and tell the truth of my life now. There is not a lot else I can do. Maybe someday truth will make a difference to this world.

Eunice wife, her name was Miss Kitty, she was a white woman, you could see by her nose and her mouth. If ever Miss Kitty see Eunice try to push labourers beyond endurance, she come up and say, 'Oh, Stafford', she call him Stafford, to his face I call him Mr Eunice, behind back we call him Stafford, 'Don't be like that, they all have to live.' And he say, 'You leave it alone, woman, this is man's business.' Eunice was a pig.

Miss Kitty and her brother look to be English, but I don't know where they from. You could not find nobody to ask those question. We could not ask any question. We was not counted.

Rich man, English man, so-call white, they put all the pressure on my people. We was coloured, I don't say black because some of us black, some brown, some yellow-skin - but we have no money, and we not white. The rich man have money, and rich man son come up and he put pressure on the labourers like father did do before, and this way he keep rich, or get richer. And poor stay poor.

In this job I must drive Eunice milk cart, which is like an English rag and bone cart. The cart carry big churns of milk, several gallon of milk in each. A man help me lift these churn onto the cart and I then drive them to the station. At the station I must carry those big churns on my own. But Eunice give me my own place to live. And he give me fourteen shilling a week!

I think maybe I will never get more than fourteen shilling a week. But something else has changed since I living with Aunt Evelyn - I find myself a woman. In those days I did not know what you call love. I did not spend time with a woman because I love her, I did not know what was love. But I am now a little bit settled with a place to live, and a woman with me. Eunice is happy. Fourteen shillings a week.

This is one of the hardest and worst positions to be in: to work and to live-in. Any time of night and day the boss come and knock on your door. Any time. And when the boss knock, you work, because if you don't work, then you have no job. And when you have no job, you have no place where you live. So I was semi-slave, I had to work and I couldn't scream. If I said anything wrong, Eunice could say 'take your bag and go.'

Eunice was nothing special, you understand. Eunice was just a man, but he had the money. And Eunice care not whether I stay or go, live or die. So I stay there for about three year. The woman I with is also working, she is doing garden work for another family that have money. She work in the vegetable garden of a house, so we have vegetable coming in, and we have a little money. I do then what I do ever since. No matter how little money I getting each week, I always keep a bit of it to save.

It take a long time, say three year, but I save a couple of pound. Enough!

I left Eunice and use the money to rent a plot of land in Spanish Town. With a bit of help I put up a 'one room and lean-to'. So I have a woman, a bit of land, and my own place to live. I am started. But I still have to work for another to get enough to live on. Now I working for two bosses. Myself and Edwin Charley.

Edwin Charley have what we call a cane piece, a sugar cane plantation, factory, estate, whatever you want to call it. There is work on this cane piece for six month of the year.

I think I moan and groan inside, in my heart, from age ten to twenty five. In them year I laugh no more than four time. But you had to keep amuse in some way, if you get miserable everything go wrong for you, and when life really hard, you cannot bear that it get harder. We boys, we young men, we play like little boy sometime, we play with cashew nuts, see how many you can throw in a hole, one who get most in keep them, daft thing like that. You see we always try to be happy, if you didn't happy with each other... you wouldn't survive. But at the same time I were very bitter then, trying to come through.

First time I start to laugh were when I found work at Edwin Charley and started to get ahead a little bit. It is hard to explain the truth, we were like the black in South Africa, money was scarce, we did not know what it were to have a couple of pound in our pocket. But when you working at Edwin Charley you get a weekly wage, and food wasn't scarce, so when Friday come, you hear your name call, and you get a wage. It were when I at Edwin Charley that I got a nice pair of trouser and first pair of proper boot on my feet. I saved up and could afford to buy a push bike. From the moment I reach work there, my life start to change, I start to be a bit happy.

Before Edwin Charley I were getting fourteen shilling a week, five o'clock in morning until five o'clock at night, sometime later, and I didn't get a bloody holiday. At Edwin Charley cane piece I get about three pound a week. This three pound a week is the result of Bustamente getting Union going. Imagine what that kind of money mean after working for Eunice.

I don't know who Edwin Charley was, I think he was Englishman, or American, but we didn't know him, we did not see him, he just like Tate and Lyle. We only know the come-betweeners, the slave drivers. But still, according to the Government they had to pay a certain wage and that was due to Bustamente. He went through pressure. He were punched and kicked, beaten and put in jail and everything, but he still come and do his job which was to start Union. Things change when the Union form. The big plantation had to keep to the Union rule, I don't think smaller places like Eunice included in this.

Explaining these things is very difficult because we never really know very much about what going on. We could only go by say-so as to what happen anywhere. I never buy a newspaper all my life in Jamaica. I get to know what is the Union when I grow up. When I younger I see big Union meeting, maybe by rum shop or at cross roads, I go along with my mates but we listen only for as long as it take to smoke a cigarette. Sometime there so many people, so much noise, you couldn't even hear. The shops were glad of these crowd, and there was no real trouble as far as I know. I never hear of no tangle with police.

These Union men who come round were all Jamaican, plenty of black men, blacker than myself. But fairest skin Union man I ever see addressing a meeting is Bustamente himself. He were about my height, which is five foot ten inch, I don't think he were any taller, but stutter. He were a nice man. He work for the poor worker and try never to let us down. When Bustamente was going round preaching and talking about Union, I was still giddyhead boy, I wasn't interested. But when I reach Edwin Charley, where the Union was, I very grateful to Bustamente.

Imagine, you out of work and you hear cane piece might take on man. And you go and there is a line of men crushed maybe over a hundred yard and broad as a road. You keep on going and you keep on hoping that you might reach the front. Slowly you advance, the land is dry, no rain, the machine is running: they take fifty men. Now molasses start to flow from machine: take on a hundred. The machine get lively we hear, and they take on a hundred and fifty!

Then come day when you go and you hear your name call out. Oh, you are the one. It like somebody call you to a gold mine! When they call you, they inspect you, the only thing left was to search mouth for your age on your teeth... semi-slavery. 'You come here! And you, come here!' This is red-face who going to pick if you work or not. When I find myself in the batch of the selected one, I start to snap my finger, and my heart feel like a piece of paper screwed up tight and the screw of the paper start to open.

You just imagine, you not getting anything before, now you expect that you might be going to get a job with a bit of wage for six month. And when they come now and say 'All right, we have enough, Finished!' Who will get picked out of the selected group? We selected still have to pass test. 'Have you been work at a cane piece before? Have you been work at factory? Which factory? For how long?' And so they sort through, examining your build, your delivery when questioned. You might look a bit weak, or maybe you can't represent who you are or where you are from or what your work is been, so they say, 'You go over there!' All the while is two group being made. And all the while it terrible in your heart, in your mind, all the time you waiting to hear the outcome of examination. And then the examination is finished.

When you find you get job... everything start to smile! Your finger smile, even your hair stand up in rejoicement. No matter what work is, you going to get wage, which is money.

I work hard at that cane piece, and every year I get work there. Through that place, and my little cultivation, I earn enough to come here to England.

So I work for Edwin Charley for some years, and for myself I am growing food and rice that I sell to the government. First I have a half an acre, then an acre, then a bit more. I rent this land in co-operation with maybe six other young lads trying to come through, it is our field to cultivate. To rent an acre for six month is about six pound.

Certain time of year, I must work on cane piece and my own land. Then life is terrible hard. I work on the cane piece until six o'clock at night, then I home for something to eat. After I eat, my working day start again with me bicycling six or seven mile to the land I rent. I work alone until three sometime even four in morning. By God we had to work hard. Rice don't grow on hilly land, rice grow on level land, and you have to have plenty water. I remember one place where we rent the land there was a few coconut tree. That land was mine by renting, but landlord exclude or exempt the coconut tree, that his. So the first place we plant rice was round coconut root! He know better than to trample our rice to get to his coconut! Anybody trample the rice know they get trouble!

Always to start planting we must first dig our land with fork. Not a tractor, just a fork in your hand. We dig our land through in this way. This the reason I have always know hard work and live by it. We fork through the field, if it not level, we level it, we have to, and we do level it with fork in our hand, no machine. When we have dug over and level the land, we make a banking, maybe nine inches, maybe higher than foot, it depend on the land. This banking run all way round the field, inside banking is divided into section according to how many of us lads are working field.

All this banking and section is for when we go to keep some water, we can store it in the field. Water, irrigation, was like gold. Rain only fall say four times a year. We might get what you call spitting, but by spitting no rice can grow. Rice must get proper soaking with water, and water were scarce.

Rice was cheap, water was not too cheap, and we did got no money to buy a big lot of water. You can say we desperate. And because we desperate we find way of getting very cheap water!

Rich man with many acre can afford to buy plenty water from irrigation company. So we try to rent land very close to a rich man land, then all his water is nearby us. This one reason I never get to bed till four o'clock in morning. The big man employ a water-man to irrigate his rice, and guard his water. This servant or worker must stop by the water to preserve it. But everybody get sleepy. I was sleepy too, but I couldn't afford to go to sleep. If I lose the rice, I am back where I started. So I watch the man until sleep or go home and when he has gone, we go to where the rich man water is kept and we pull the dam down.

Remember we are working this in groups, but what you might call, self-employ. One of us pull the dam down and the water coming like a small river. So we direct the water, the small river, into our field. Then we sit down there and watch the water going through, from bank to bank, section to section. Maybe this start at eleven at night, when the watch-man cannot hold on any longer, because he working all day. I working all day too, I working at Edwin Charley cane piece, but this is my only hope of getting my head through.

I remember when the water first come into a section it melt like the sun hit butter, the land just suck up the water. And when it had enough, we send the water on to next section. To grow rice you must give the land a proper soak, so that it can hold no more water. This land is loam on top and have clay bottom, when it soak it hold water for long time, maybe month. Maybe for a crop of rice we must do this action four or five times. The rich man know what we doing, he realise. If we steal enough water at night for our land, he have water all day and every day to irrigate his land.

You must understand, for you to get anywhere you have to be determined, and fight like Hell. We was that way. We were not getting rich, we were fighting just for survival. Rich man know that if we decide to break that dam tonight and he did come along... we bust his head with stone. He was whiteman, little red-skin man, which is so-call white man, only big when he up on back of big horse! Sometime he might see us break his dam, but mostly he in bed with his wife when we do it. White man in Jamaica never work night and day. He never need to work night and day. Even if he see water flow from his land, he think it best to look the other way, just one man against five young boys. He wouldn't have a chance. If he fetch the police, the police wouldn't help him. And, if he fetch police, he know soon he wouldn't have no plant, nothing. Police wouldn't want to know.

This wasn't England. Those days the police they say, 'We not here to protect rice planters'. And how you think police going to protect this water? I tell you, at night it so dark you could hold the darkness in your hand. You think the police going to left the road, which is nearly as dark, to come down maybe one mile into a man property, just for the theft of water? Police not know who waiting for him there. In that dark a man could be hurted and don't know how it happen! And police is rare. We have what you call Area Constable and you see him about as often as you see a Bishop. Most policing done by informer who try to get palm greased one way or other, we call these people pan-head. Pan-head is so loved that if he cry out at night he answered with a stone! They was corrupt and they was the enemy of ordinary people. Pan-head go round in a group for fear of attack. I know pan-head got the backs of their leg cut in that dark; bloke wait for him come by on horse, then rush out and cut his leg with cutlass. When people under pressure you get some damn funny thing happen.

Anyway, we only thief that water at night. It could be hard and cold, working the water at night, specially when you been working cane piece all day. It a lot of pressure for a young man. But this was a way of trying to come through and make something of life.

These real bad days I must be at the cane piece

at six in the morning. Between my rice field and the cane piece I have time only for coffee, good, real coffee (we had not any tea when I were a young man), some food, and very little sleep.

I know you can't live like this for long. As I become more tired, I have to fall back and start later at the cane piece, but then I come home later. Some morning I late, some night I late. If I am to work I must get some little sleep. That the way my life to run for many years in Jamaica.

I learn this during those years: the rich kind of people get rich, the rich kind of people stay rich. And I look about me today, in England, in 1987 and I think this: for the poor people, this country is becoming like the West Indies. So now I tell you how we used to make coffee!

This is how we make real coffee when I were a kid, and real coffee were the only coffee we know. First we have coffee growing, so we collect the red coffee berry and let sun dry out juice. Then we break shell of berry and take out the two beans, these we roast on a sort of grill. The same mortar we use to break the shell, we use to beat and break and grind the beans. It take a long time, but you make the beans into a powder as fine as flour. The flour you put in a big pot and boiling water go in after. You let it stand, then you add milk. Another way for making coffee, if you don't make the beans into a fine powder, is put the ground beans into a cloth bag and put that in boiling water for six or seven minute. But why do we put sugar in coffee? Now I sometime wonder why we do buy coffee; buy it bitter, then you put so much sugar in to make it sweet. They say if you in Rome you do as Romans do. And in England, no matter what you used to do in Jamaica, you forget, and now I do make my coffee English way.

So that's how I make good, strong coffee in the morning before I go to the cane piece. The work I did then I couldn't do now. We had a removable line. An iron line like for a railway, but on this line we have carts which are pulled by cow or ox. The line is laid and all the cane near it is cut and taken to this cart to be carried to the cane piece factory. When all that cane is cut and moved, the line is moved to another part of the cane piece. Cutters are paid by the ton, paid for what they do. But if you working the line, you paid by the ton that come off the line. It can be better working the line, but you have to work hard and fast to make your pay. I was young and strong. In the morning I go and I told, today you working on the line, after a while I working the line all the time.

There is good going and bad going. When everything going smooth, you that working on the line don't have to do too much work. But sometime it a wetty week and the line is sloppy and the cow is muddy and under pressure... then you must come and do what's needed. Maybe you just have to push the truck all day. Maybe the truck did not move, maybe it capsided, it don't matter, you still have to find time to load the truck again and again, because all that cut cane is piling up and piling up. This work is constant pressure.

So, if you are cutter you are an all round man, and you working for yourself. But if you are on the line you're working with a group of men. If we don't put hands on heart together...there is no wage. What we must do is muck in. Life on the line wasn't great, but I known worse. I known things I can hardly think to write about. I not so old, but I have seen horse-whip used on a man because he did slow down from tired or weakness. But Union was being organised, there was a chance that things going to get a bit better. Wage wasn't great, but, now I find, all in all, I getting more than fourteen shilling a week!

I'm just passing twenty, I have a few pounds, and I'm more considerate now. I have a little house, I living with a woman. We both very young, but I starting to think better. I am more settled. I work at the cane piece and I cultivate my rice. I don't run street and be giddyhead no more. Truth is, I have not time to run street and be giddyhead no more.

It take time, but I save enough money to have two head of cow and a bicycle. In those day a cow and calf cost about £7.50, now my brother, who still live in Jamaica, tell me he must pay about £200 for a good cow and calf. Things move!

I keep my cow and maybe a calf on the little plot of land around my house. The little feed I have there is not enough, so at night I go out and cut guinea grass again. But now I can tie bundles of grass on my bicycle to bring them back and chop up for the cow. The cow give good milk. Six month on the cane piece, six month on the rice. Hard work, but I young and strong. Everything fine.... but it take fifteen years of work like this for me to save enough to pay the fare to this country of England.

You ask me: Why come to England? I tell you, that a question I ask myself a thousand time since I come here. All I do now is tell how it come about. I do try to understand my life, how things have work out. But before telling how I come to England, I go back to my school days and my childhood in Mountainside.

TWO

CHILDHOOD DAYS

They say the child is father to the man so, afore I go on with my life as a working man, I tell you something about my school days. I was a bugger, you know. I was a bugger, and that's the reason I'm not too good at reading. The moment I get to school, see the other kids trailing about in the yard, I bugger off, into the fields and woods. I spent most of my school days up a tree, and I'm disgracing myself telling this, but it's the truth.

It was me alone, a kid, a little kid, what I done didn't help me then, and I shamed of it still. I don't read paper now, it's of little use to me. If I want to know what's on the television, I ask my son, and it is he reads out and tells me. When I was nine and it come to schooling, I tell you, I didn't know a bull foot from a cow foot. But back in the West Indies it were hard as a kid, coming through.

You see I come from a place they call Mountainside, it not a village more of an area. And what we called the street was not street like here in England; street in Jamaica were a rough road of stone, no tar. When it wet, the street is made of stone and water. Mountainside was a farming area, tenant farmers with maybe ten to thirty acre each. I think most houses were built in the middle of plots, on high land if there is high land, so the farmer can see the land. There a lot of space between what you call neighbour. When I a kid I can stand outside my father house and holler as loud as I can, and nobody hear me who isn't in that house. Some of the wood round Mountainside is so thick you can't move in it. And some kids live so far away from school (which is in a church) that they just never ever go. Or they have a father who say, 'Boy, you not need reading and writing.' I think my father want me to read and write because he and mother had a little bit of reading... maybe as much as I have now.

So it were the late nineteen twenties and I attain the age of seven, which is when we are starting to go to school. The first two years were just to get you used to the idea of schooling. I was always hiding away, truth is, I never really get use to idea of schooling.

Your parents can only say No! when you are in their sight. Where I grow up no longer you step out of yard and you are out of sight. It were like jungle. Guinea grass and bush were higher than I was. Right off, as very little boy, I learn to climb tree, you had to, to see what was going on. I tell you already how at this age I work with my father's animal before I supposed to go to school. When I get home from that work my mother say for me to get ready now and go to school. This I do, and I walk out of home as if I going to school. But I just go on past school, sometimes I didn't even walk in that direction. And my sister, she is much smaller than me, and we live that good together that she always cover up for me.

At first I went to school, and the truth is that I did like that school. But the teacher was very rough, very mean; drastic I would say.

The head teacher was call Mr Simms. He were about five foot six, very dark skin, call him black. Some say we all black, but Mr Simms were very black. Where he from I don't know. His wife was a bit more yellow-skin woman, and she wasn't too bad. But he were a bugger. Mr Simms it were who first encourage me to keep away from school!

Every day you had to know your lesson, what people here call 'homework'. You do this little lesson at home and take it into school on the next day. Well I didn't get no time for this homework, all my time were taken up on looking after my father horse and goat and so on. And when I finish my day, which start at five or six in the morning and don't finish till seven or eight at night, I did not think about homework, I did think about some play. I were only seven so I had to go out a do a bit of playing.

So, next morning, after doing my work with father animals, I in school and I have not done my homework. Then I get the cane. And I did get cane. Many time. And I do not mean sugar cane, I mean beating on the hand so they bruise and hurt. The answer seem to me to be... don't go to school.

After that, most of the time I just didn't go. As I get near the school I see the teacher drilling the kids in the yard, making them march. I look at them, and I think how Mr Simms will cane me, and I walk past and turn into the first field I find. But I can't go too far from school, because I had to go home for my dinner at twelve o'clock. The only way I could know what going on, and be home so mother don't know I'm not going to school, is to watch the school from the tallest tree around. That's why I say I spend most of my school days up a tree!

About ten to twelve each day the kids in school did sing a song, and that let me know that it time to go home for dinner and I say to myself, 'All right, they singing a song, it about time I come down out of this tree.' But I didn't spend all my time up the tree. I come down and do my different rounds. I had play and stuff to get on with. You see we did not have no clock, I tell time by looking at my shadow. I look at my shadow and I know when it near enough twelve because my shadow is under my feet. As my old people let me know, when you walking on your shadow, it nearly twelve o'clock. So I always back up the tree when I think it just before twelve, make sure I see when other kids are going home

By the time the kids were passing my home, I was going in for my dinner, so mother didn't know what I doing. And when they went back to school, I didn't go back to school. I went back to my same old woods where I am picking fruit, eating one bite, then throwing away. And there is fruit in Jamaica: mango, cashew, plum, orange, a lot more. I use fruit as ball, kick it around, just to keep the time going while the other kids is in school. I set traps to catch birds and animals. All sort of practice I do to keep time passing. And then sometime I get bored and try school again.

Monday I always start out to go. Monday night I get homework. Tuesday I might go to school and try excuse for not having my homework. Wednesday I never go. I think then I was doing myself good. I wasn't. I was cutting my own throat.

Well I continue like this until my father catch me. What happen is somebody see me in the woods and tell my father. My father ask me, 'Is this true?' And I own it to him. I remember it now: I did get a proper flogging for hiding away. So I try to go to school and keep going to school, but then, because I don't do my lessons, I did get a proper flogging from Mr Simms. It all seem too much for me, so I make complaint and I make complaint till at last father take me away from that school.

Now I go to a new school and there is only me from where I live at this school, but it near where my father work, so he can keep eye on me. And for dinner I must go to a neighbour, because it too far for me to travel home.

Well, I did go to that neighbour for my dinner, but did I go to the new school? I did not. I find another tree! So it were the same routine for a time. Then something happen to go wrong for me.

What I forget is my father eye. Soon he see me in my tree when I should be in school. Before he can catch me, I run from him. I run into the woods because I afraid of what he will do. But at some hour

43

I must come in to my home because the truth is that I afraid of the dark.

In Jamaica where I were living then, we have no lights at night, only the blinkies, what you call fireflies. When there is no moon or stars, the dark is round your eye like a black cloth. You see nothing. You see not which is up or down. When it this dark and the blinkies open up and give light for a split second, it a chance to see where is the road. The houses are very far apart, and even the house only lit with kitchen bitch which is a sort of kerosene lamp giving sooty little flame. I see a lot of people who lose a hand or arm from the kitchen bitch, because it is dangerous. If a child knock against it, he get burning kerosene on him, and it can burn into say the elbow. The parent treat this burn with a local remedy, but the skin and flesh set solid, and that child can no longer bend his arm, or use is hand. I had trouble once cause by kitchen bitch. I see Father have a bottle hid and sometime he take a swig from it. So one day I look everywhere and find the bottle... I think. But what I find is kerosene bottle. I take swig and then scream all way to kitchen. For a week my mouth hurt me. Only the well off people have paraffin lamps with mantle and glass.

So Mountainside people have kitchen bitch in the house, blinkies outside. Not much light. They always say there are ghosts walking about at night. Now I never see any ghost, and I don't believe in ghost... but I always get in before dark, maybe some stray ghost get me! I still little boy, remember.

So I go home, afraid of dark, afraid of Father. I listen careful and don't hear Father. I think he sleeping. I have no key to house, which is thatch house, walls of wire netting plastered with sand and cement. Front of the house have two windows, and one of these window is always off the catch. I lift the window, quiet, and I climb into the house. Maybe he hear me at the window, I don't know... but he not sleeping!

My father ask me what I was doing up tree. This time I give him any answer, I don't own up what I doing out of school, last time he give me a flogging so I more careful now. And I get another bloody clapping because he know I make an excuse and am telling him a lie.

So it flogging at home and flogging at school. I look at this and I think I have to be at home, but I don't have to be at school. I decide I might as well make do with home flogging.

So to my way of thinking then, my school days is over and this I tell my father. In the end he decide he will just leave me alone. And he did leave me alone. Now I look back and I think he decide to leave me alone about school because he know that someday I going to be sorry. And by God, he were right. Today I am ashamed to go to church even. I would like to go to church and sing the hymns, but I can't read fast enough to keep up. And I think he leave me alone because I am the only boy at this time and I looking after his animal and doing work for him and it cost him nothing. So I left school and I didn't know much, and I didn't care much.

It were a few year later that I come to understand what I done. I were working for one shilling a day. I was sick of it. My first cousin was always luckier than me, he was working as Sanitary Inspector in Spanish Town and he find a way to go to America. As a first cousin, he pass his job over to me. It were a good job that would pay me a reasonable wage for those days. When he take me to the office and explain, the people there was feeling all right about me having the job. But when the pen and paper come down on the table I couldn't go half way to writing a statement... I couldn't even sign my name properly. It was the first time I regret my schooldays. I were seventeen or thereabouts. All I done during my schooldays was play with the birds and animal and fruit. Climb my tree. That the reason I started life like I daft, and I end up like I daft.

The truth is that the few days I did go to school, I only go to play. Kids here sometime get a cog out of a clock or watch and make what they call spinning top, we call this a gig. We make a cotton reel gig out of what you call a cotton bobbin. The bobbin we have then were tin, about two inch long, and with flat tin ends, about half of an inch across. What you do first is cut the bobbin end off, with about half inch of spindle. Next you need a pencil, this where school come in. We lads know where there is always about six pencil! Teacher have them for when we write. Whenever teacher go out, or we get anywhere near desk, we try to get a pencil. Everyone always want a pencil. We don't get these pencil to write, we need the pencil point! We push the pencil through the bobbin end, and the pencil give us a good point for the gig to spin on, and a handle at the top to spin with. A gig with a pencil point spin a lot longer.

Of course teacher always wonder how we take advantage, who got all the pencil when he out. This is what we do. We always have a nail or something on us, and with this nail we have made a little hole in the board floor of the school, a knot hole, you call it. Under the floor is a small cellar where nobody ever go... except us little boys. We drop pencil down this hole. When teacher try to get his pencils back he search all our boys, he know it not the girls, it was the boys. Sometime he find maybe two pencil out of that half a dozen, and sometime he find none. As far as I know teacher must think on many occasion, 'How the Hell the pencil gone and I can't find any pencil on the boys.' But we had know since the first time he search us, and find all the pencil, we must find a way to get pencil out of school. That is why we make that hole in the floor boarding.

You might think that a lot of trouble to make a gig, but you remember we have few thing in the school, and we was that poor that father never think of giving a plaything or toy. He have to think about buying some clothes or buying some food. When at school we play near teacher yard, because he might send us for some fruit or something. We go to his house quite happily: we look around all the time, eye darting in case we find something, a boot polish tin, a piece of cloth or cord, anything that could make a toy.

47

We had a big playground, you could run for about two hundred yard and we did do running and jumping, which I like. I jump very good. And at school there was plenty of boys and we did a lot of fighting. I liked to be in the battle, fighting!

Like I say the head teacher is called Mr Simms, and he have two middle teacher who are women. You'd hardly find a school in Jamaica with three women teacher, they always need one man. Plenty of the boys was bigger than the teacher by the time they reach fourteen, and they was unruly, even to a man. West Indian kids grow fast, and they depend on the woods; we could do anything, then jump off into the woods and get away.

I remember one day we have a bit of trouble in the school. We decide we will have a big fight about four o'clock. The reason was this. Some big boys in the school live on the right side of the street, but they always coming on the left side, following girls who live on our side! Moving into our area. So, we boys on the left side decide that we will fight to stop these other boys following our girls, moving on our side of the street. I think, 'These right side boy, they really taking advantage!' To me, then, it were very important.

At that school we had slates for learning to write. I soon follow the others and I take the wood from round my slate and now my slate is a weapon for protection! Never mind learn to write, I use my slate for slapping and chopping. Soon there is a big battle. Things are getting very rough and my slate catch one of the boys from the right. He makes a lot of noise.

Mr Simms get to hear of what has happen, but I did not think that I will get a whipping for it. Next morning I make a big mistake. I go to school!

The teachers call us all up to find out what all the uproar was about last night after school. Whether it right or wrong, everybody hand it on to me. Truth was it were me had hit the other boy with the slate, but it were not only me that been chopping at boys with slate.

Mr Simms give me the cane. Six lashes. Six lashes on my right hand. Then he decide to give my six lashes on my left hand also. I tell him he can't. It good enough that he damage one hand. I were about fourteen, and strong enough at this time to put up some defence He grab my collar and we struggle. He shaking me, but I didn't give him my left hand. Lucky I was far away from my slate. If I could have reached my slate I would have chopped that teacher. But not letting him lash me another six, it just make it worse for me in school. And this was another reason I didn't have much time for that place. It's all over, I think, and I finished school before my time. I regret it now, but at that time I just did not care; school did not seem sensible place to be.

*

So now I've told you about some of my work and some of my school days. But it weren't all work and hiding from school, I liked to do a bit of playing as well.

My father just couldn't afford to give me very much. I was the first boy, I don't know now what he give my younger brother, the last born, for I were away from home by then. I remember that when I were about five, I start to think about having something to play with like a toy. I was shy of asking my father for anything such as a toy to play with. Moreover, I never seen any kid with a toy, but I just want something to play with, anything. One day I pick up some boot polish tin from the place where well off people were living. Anything such as polish tin were good to find, I never did see boot polish tin in my parent house because we didn't have no bloody boots! Anyway, I decide to make something with these polish tin. What I did do is to nail these two polish tin onto ends of a piece of wood. Then a nail on two more piece of wood and I tie strings from one of these to the wheels. What I made was a sort of fragile pushing toy which I could steer, turning this way or that.

That the way I got my first toy. It was very delicate. I play with that around the area of my house, and I enjoy it very much. I were around six year old at this time.

Another toy I make from the limb of a tree. I go in the wood, the bush, and I cut the limb of a tree. I use an old, broken machete, a full machete would be too heavy for me at this time. Anyway, then I start to chop away and carve a gig. You chop the wood to something like a turnip shape, and into the point you put a nail. Then we use a special string which we have, it called English cord, we wind this string round the nail and up part of the wood. Snap the cord and the gig spins. I can pick it up, with my fingers under the nail, toss it and catch it on my hand. Run about, shout: Keep spin! Keep spin!

From early day I remember my great grandmother, she were a nice old lady. She had white hair and wear a long skirt with two string around her waist, and a blouse over it. My father grandmother, her name was Mary, She would be over eighty when I was eight, and she could walk no more than two mile without tired.

I remember well that she had big star apple tree beside her house. I don't know how they call this tree here, I don't see star apple grow in England. Enough to know they sweet and very sticky. I were somebody who like to follow Great Grandmother when she come by my house. When I were big enough to climb the star apple tree she take me to her house. I pick what I could, she take her share, and she give me some for myself, and some to take home. But I never take any home. From the moment I get through the gate I start to eat them, maybe three or four are left for my sisters.

The only joke with this star apple is it were a thing so sticky. The more you eat the more it form sticky muck around your mouth. It were a damned job to get my face clean, maybe an hour scrubbing.

I don't remember much about Great Grandmother Mary, except she were lovely and she used to smoke a little white chalk pipe. Most of what I remember she

say was things like: be a good boy... don't be rude...
that sort of thing. And Father and Mother always tell
me, 'You must talk the truth'. But as the years go by,
I get flogged for talking the truth, so I become a bit
more careful. I learn that if in a corner, it better to say
'about' instead of the exact truth.

When I were about eleven, the thing I like best
was to be playing in the woods near my home. We
didn't have no toy to play with, only the few thing we
make, so I had to find my own activity to do. I enjoy
stoning fruit. The woods in Jamaica have many fruit
tree of all kinds and I am interested to see how far
and how straight I can fling a stone. So my practice
is to see a mango or a pear, and see how many stone
I need fling before I hit it off the tree. Sometime I
might not be too good, knock a lot of fruit off the tree
before I hit the one I after.

Mainly I stone the neighbour's fruit tree. If I stone
father's tree I going to get flogged. I remember one
day I see a lovely pear, it were a pear that the sun
burnt, it look reddish. I wanted that pear, it look so
lovely. I stone away, trying to get that red pear. Then
the neighbour come. I run like hell and scale the
fence. I away and the neighbour can't catch me. But
the neighbour smart. He pick up all the fruit from
underneath the tree, put them in a bag, and take
them to my father. 'It your boy that hitting all the fruits
off me tree,' he say.

When my father ask me about it, I own it and say
'yes, I done it'. He ask me why I done it. I tell him how
I saw one pear which is right lovely and reddish with

the burning of the sun. And I tell him how much I wanted that one, and how before I could get that one, there was a lot on the floor.

He say, 'Why you do it?' And I say, 'I tell you why.' And I get another damned flogging.

I used to tell the truth, but I don't promise anyone since some of those floggings that I really have much stomach for telling the truth. Kids never learn. He always tell me, 'Boy, you must talk the truth'. Now when I think of all the grown up, parent, teacher, saying tell truth, tell truth I think they might not know it, but they tell me a lot of lies, but that is something I explain later.

Kids is kids and I sometime curse kids for doing what I used to do myself. But some of the thing we do in Jamaica make me unhappy when I think of them. I wonder why I ever need to do such thing. There a kind of lizard live in the West Indies. He climbs about in the trees and is about half foot long. If I with another boy and I see one of these lizard, we try and find another and catch them both. This is how we catch him. We take a stalk of guinea grass, which is hollow, and we thread certain stringy bark or cord through, so that it form a kind of noose. The lizard just sit on his tree, sometime he hanging upside down by his feet, which have little claws for him to grip with. We put the noose over his head and pull him down.

So we have a lizard each, fastened tight by the throat at the end of a noose. Now we push them at each other to make a fight. I don't know how we so cruel, but we was boys and we seen this what big boys do. It hurt me now to remember such play. Sometime at night I remember lizard fight, and I just want to hide that remembrance from myself.

Young kid need all sorts to keep them occupy. I remember we had two men who used to do sawing when certain tree fall, or sometime they come and cut down tree. That's the way West Indies people get board for house. We didn't have no money to go in town and buy board. If there was town where board was available for purchase I didn't know of it. First time I see them cutting up tree for board was when I realise it must be that way Daddy get board for house we all living in.

They come with a horse and cart. A big horse, I never see a small horse before I come to England. The cart is like a rag and bone cart, but the wheel are much bigger, this is to carry away the boards. This is how they cut the board. First they cut the tree down and take off the branches, now they are left with a log. I remember they have a scaffold and they have a real hard time getting big log on this scaffold. So that the scaffold not too high, they dig a hole underneath for a man to stand in. This hole is deep so that he not too near the log, and there is space for saw. I remember the first time I see these men doing there work, it look stupid to me. One man going around this big log with some strings and a piece of iron on the end, and coal, or chalk for making mark on the wood. They was taking measurement, and I wonder what the Hell they taking measurement for. And when they cut the first piece it is very rough. The second piece they cut is better. But then they are cutting lovely board, straight, lovely board.

This was very interesting for me to watch, but what I remember best about this sawing business is that they always cook their special food for dinner on a little fire. I guess they employ by rich person to chop the tree and sell the board they make. They could be there for a month, they could be there for two month. But where they come from? I didn't interested where they come from or any such question. I was just interested to see the pot was on the fire.

I think they was glad of the company. They was working, and they had to work hard, and they did work hard.

Mostly what they cook is flour dumpling and bits of pork in thin gravy or soup. Well, flour was one of the scarcest thing in the West Indies, next to money. It were there, but you couldn't make it, you had to buy it. There was not a lot of money, so flour was scarce for us. We did have corn, but it sweet corn, and that makes corn meal, not flour. Corn meal alone could not be kneaded for good dumpling.

Everyday that these sawyers were working in our area, I did try to get there by dinner time. There were not things I could do to help. I couldn't pull that big saw, but I stand there and watch. They were big man, they didn't mind giving me some food. They give me one dumpling. I still see them flour dumpling, I still can taste them flour dumpling. When they give me one dumpling it were a proper dumpling, they didn't make them little thing you call dumpling in this country, them make big flour dumpling, as broad as palm of a man hand and twice as thick.

And pork, it true we had pork, but mostly round Christmas. We couldn't afford to kill one pig every month. We had to take care of our pig, because a pig weighing, say, four stone, you'd only get three shilling for it. You had to sell a lot of pig to get say, a set of clothes for a family. So pork was quite scarce, but flour was double scarce. I always try and get there about half past eleven. We didn't have no clock, I tell time by looking at my shadow. I always check how close my shadow was to my feet, and if it getting late, I run like hell to get to the sawyers before they eat all their food.

That pork he cook with the dumpling, kids nowadays would say, 'Why you giving that water with bits in to me?', but I didn't mind because it were that nice to me then. I don't know why, but now, in all my retainance, or memory, I didn't ever get corn and flour dumpling. When I recall my days as young kid I always get pure flour dumpling, and that the reason I follow these two men when they come to cut board out of tree. They was nice men, kind.

It was very nice if anyone come along and give me half a penny, which were two farthing

With money such as this you could get sweetie: three mint ball for a farthing. It not every week that a kid could afford a pennyworth of mint ball. And you could get biscuit for money also, special kind of cracker which taste right good. For three farthing you get a dozen of these cracker. Imagine how much a kid would enjoy that, maybe you never get a dozen biscuit for two month. When you a kid who get no regular money, and maybe just a couple of farthing after two or three week of nothing, buying three farthing of biscuit... it must be really important.

When we do come up with a gill, which is what we call three farthing, well it something for a kid to be very happy about, like a kid a pound or more now. We did not get many gill when we kid. But maybe sometime Grandma come along and give us a gill, then we rich for a week! A little bit make us happy, because we don't have a lot. In them day the money all come from England, we had ten shilling paper over there, like here. The farthing have a little bird on it, we had a little bird like that one. The half penny have ship on it. When it come to thinking concerning coming to England I were glad that England have same money as Jamaica, but farthing worried me. How could a rich country need farthing?

One thing I say about the West Indies when I were a boy, we never go hungry. We can get any amount of food, but there's not a lot of kids have more than one pair of trouser. And if a kid have more than one trouser, then he have a pair that he never wear, these is reserve trousers and the one he wear is probably just bits of a pair of trouser.

No kids is hungry for the reason that the woods is full of trees with fruit that we can eat. The land is so good that anything grow there. And plants grow all year round, no need for them to sleep through winter like they must do in England. We have no winter and autumn in Jamaica. We just have summer. Throw down tiny bit of banana root and soon there is banana tree, and soon it heavy with ripe banana. A kid could eat and eat and never need to remember that there is kitchen at home. But clothes and shoes don't grow on trees.

I remember how father and the neighbours go hunting for food in the wood. Maybe ten farmer with a lot of dogs, seventy or eighty. And they take mules, but first they wrap any old cloth or clothing round the mule. They tie all this padding on, then they tie wicker-work all around the mule, so that he well protected. Last they put big wooden saddle on him, to carry home what they going to catch.

They out after boar, not little piggy, but big boar with tusk that can stab through a man. Sometime they go out with near a hundred dog and come home with twenty. Most farmer have a lot of dogs, twenty or more, just run around the area of house and farm. They like kids, off on rounds in the wood, hunting mongoose or cat, or anything they can catch. And they fed by throwing anything left over into a trough. Out of our dogs, two were named dogs; call for Breeze Mark or Seek and Dive, and they come with all the dogs. The other dogs had no name, but as they roam it mean that nobody stray on a farmer land.

Seek and Dive was a big, smooth hair dog, tan in colour and with black patch over each eye. I really fancy Seek and Dive for my own dog, he was my favourite and he travel about with me when I play in the woods. Maybe he was a bit smart, and Breeze Mark: they never killed by boar.

Maybe the boar run until he tired out, maybe he stop and fight straight away. If he stop and fight, then a lot of dogs get killed and damaged by his tusks.

It the dogs that kill the boar in the end. The men spend a week or more in the deep woods, sleep in shelter made from thatch leaves, in this time they could catch maybe five boar, big animal that stand up to a man's waist. There enough meat to keep the families for more than a month. So hunting bring good meat for people, but it never bring shoes or trouser! For this you need money, and money is always short.

My father have three or four breed mares and when it come Christmas time he can sell a mule. With the money from this sale my mother go to store and pay last year bill, then she get cloth to make next year clothes for us all. This was how it was, you pay the cloth for this year, and you make the clothes for next year. At the end of the year you must sell something to pay, then you get cloth for the year after. It were hand to mouth living. Putting it another way, it were struggling to keep your bottom from public view!

I remember the first shirt I ever buy for myself. I were older by then, living in Spanish Town, playing giddyhead. This shirt were lovely, white silk with blue flowers on the pocket - I pride it a lot. Japanese shirt. First time I put on this shirt is to go to the pictures. You see I a young man, working, and I try to enjoy myself. A special show was coming, The Ten Commandments, and I hear that Moses is in this picture.

This is a picture I really want to see. All during my childhood I told about what happen in Bible, now I can see if it true. That were how I was thinking.

When I get there to the picture house, the queue is very long. But I a young man, determined, and I rough; being this way I find myself about fifth position in the queue. Where I stand, close to the door, is a piece of wire that hang down from the corner of the building. I hook myself onto the wire, I wrap it round my hand. You can tell from this that queuing for the pictures in them days can be a bit rough!

When they open the door of the picture house, the queue start to push forward. I hold on. Fifth place and in my new Japanese shirt: I feel good. The queue start to surge from the back. But my hand is hooked to the wire. All they do is push me forward and when they relax, I fall back into the same position where I were. So, in the end I am fifth into the picture house, where there are no lights on. But when they put the lights up I see what happened to my silk shirt with the blue flowers on the pocket. I still have the neck, and the front isn't too bad, but at the back is just a little piece left, hanging down. That was the first shirt I ever buy, which I loved, and I didn't know when I able to buy another one. It were torn to bits.

Ten Commandments were the first nice picture I go to see and I get my shirt torn off my back. My pair of trouser were near as bad.

So in them early years I run giddyhead at home, then in Spanish Town. I explain to you concerning women. When we reach a certain age, we start to see girls, and we start to see the shapes of girls. And they were all smashing. We try to get in the company of all the girls, thereby sorting them out.

This kind of approach went on. It went on for a while, then I start to think and I ask myself, 'Why sorting them out? What any one got that another don't have?' So I decide it time to stop being giddyhead and trying to get mixed up with all the girls. I decide to just pick one. I think other young men is just the same.

People talk about love. I never love no woman or girl from eighteen up to thirty. I didn't know what is love. And I didn't know what is love because I didn't want to know what is love. Anyone who walk around and look a bit nice, I wanted to know if herself was as nice as she look and as she walk. So I follow her for days, and weeks, and months sometime... just to find out what she really like. One time I walk for hours through the dark, just to stand and look at the house where somebody live!

Well, when I become say twenty five to thirty, I decide that's no life. And then, just as I beginning to know what is life really like... I leave Jamaica and come to England.

THREE

BETWIST AND BETWEEN

Some people come to England and tell lies about being from rich family. I tell you, rich people kids haven't been to England, unless they come learning Doctor or some top grade education. I think some West Indian people that come to England is ashamed of their ways of life before they come here. But there is no need to be shamed of what you can't help. If nobody talk this out, tell what life were like, explain why ordinary man like me leave Jamaica for life in England, there won't be anyone know what West Indies was like all them year ago. I don't say it isn't a lot better now, with brick houses and electricity and plumbing. But I tell what I know, which is how I live before I come to England. And I tell what I see. One thing I see with my own eye is Jamaican men return from war in Europe, and another thing I see is Greenhill.

Some of my people fight in that awful war in Europe, and some of them never come home, and some come home and they mad, shell-shock we told. They live in the mad house because they can't live out of it. And many return with only one arm, only one leg, only one eye. That were an awful war. When these poor men come back, the government, which is controlled by England - Mother Country, we are told to call her - the government say any man who fight in that war will be given some land for himself, so that he can farm for the rest of his life.

So these men are given land on Greenhill. I seen Greenhill. Men who have land before they go to war see Greenhill and they turn round and walk away. I tell you, to reach your plot you must crawl on hand and knee! And if you slip you fall right back down again. Greenhill is fit for nothing but maybe a few goat. You can't grow on Greenhill and you can't graze milk cow or raise horse or mule. These men risk life for the Mother Country, they give arms and legs and eyes. And what Mother Country give them? I tell you, land on Greenhill where little will grow.

But everybody say that things is good in England. England is the Mother Country, it flow with milk and honey. It must be good there, I think, a country flowing with milk and honey.

You see we had it hard in Jamaica. Even the young women have it hard. We young lads fight for survival, but the girls have to wait until someone get his head through a little before she can get a bit of betterment. For a girl could only get security from someone else.

All my life in Jamaica people is telling me, Come to England. Come to Mother Country, it flow with milk and honey. Van come around with a film show in it: Come to England. Come to Mother Country, which flow with milk and honey.

I shamed to tell how many toe-nail I have lost from walking barefoot. The sole of your feet is harden by walking without protection, but still, you run, and a nail is torn off. In the Mother Country there is no bare-foot, no more torn away off nail. This must be a good country, I think. And we told: 'Look after Mother Country like she look after you'.

So, as I say, we were told Mother Country were running with milk and honey. That were a lie. But if a rich white man come to Jamaica, what did he find? He find he come to a milk and honey country. My country was just that, a milk and honey country for the white.

When they come along in the West Indies, they make my parents look like fool who can't handle things. But it not like that. The white man come along, and he can come small, maybe riding a push bike, just a couple of pound in pocket is enough. In a short while he rent a house, a nice house. The house and the bike let me think, 'Oh he loaded'. But the house isn't his, it rented from rich white man. Most rich white man sympathise with the white bloke. All whiteman live in house that look nice from the outside; I don't know about the inside because it not my place, I dare not go by the steps even…

Cut it short and come to the point: in a couple of year that small two pound white man have load of cow playing in the field, and he have a little car. Well, we were still walking bare-foot. As a young man I see this happen. So, here is a bit of history. If a white men is there, and if another white man come along, they quick to give him a start and so he soon moving ahead. A poor man such as my father, or myself, we have to work hard and long to stay where we was. But I did know where I was.

I was settle, working at Edwin Charlie, and coming through, things not perfect for me, but I had know worse. My people had live for long time without going to Mother Country. To give another idea of how we live I will tell about doctor treatment or medicine for ordinary poor people. Nearest doctor was nine or ten mile off in Black River Town. He pass through Mountainside once a week, on Friday. He have certain special place to stop. If you want doctor to come to you, you must put somebody out on street to wave he down as he drive through in his car. This doctor was black, I never did see no white doctor or red face doctor in Jamaica.

In those days, say thirty years ago, doctor cheapest first charge would be five pounds. So if your father didn't have five pounds in his hand, it would be useless to put a kid out to stop the doctor. When he approach the house, before he look at the patient, doctor look for five pound in the hand. The patient could be half dead, but the doctor walk away if there is no five pound. And if he take the five pound, I believe he might come back each week, and he would want five pound every time.

We had no five pound, and so what we had to do with friends or our own family was to give medicine to ourselves. We got certain bush, certain root which will help with say headache or flu or malaria. They chop and cut up things, some of it for medicine that you drink, some for bath or steam bath, boil in a big pan and breath the steam.

If you got a cut we used to use the juice of a tree. This tree they call Basida and they get the sap by cutting away the bark of the tree, then, with something like spoon, they scrape out a sticky glue or sap. We have another thing, a berry, that we call busy, it was like grated coconut, but dark. They mix the sap and the grated busy together. They wash the wound, however big, then they hold the cut tight and press the mixture all over that wound, and they tie it with a cloth bandage. After it stuck for a week or so it become hard, you could take the bandage off and leave it like that. As it get well a sort of crust form and bit fall off over time. You never see that cut again, it heal, but it leave a blue wemp a sort of scar like a ridge.

I got some of these wemp on cut that in England would be stitch and heal flat. If I catch one of these scar, knock it, it still hurt. But that the way we deal with bad cut in Jamaica.

Biggest trouble were malaria. For this we use bush, root and branches of certain trees. I don't say malaria doctored by family doctor, such as parents, is safe way, or give a proper cure, but it eases the patient and it the best we could do, because we didn't have no money for doctor.

If your eye is giving trouble, we had no eye chemist or optician, we had certain leaves and oil. This is the way I see my people survive. They take a leaf of bush, maybe the leaf we call Leaf of Life, and warm it by the fire. Then we put something like castor oil on this leaf and press it onto the eye like eye patch. You just keep leaf of life there until the eye

69

problem is well, if the leaf dry up before problem over, warm another leaf and replace dry one.

Now sometime your parent may say, 'Well, he not making no progress. We have to pay now." But they don't pay doctor, they go to person some would call witch doctor, but that is ignorant; I don't call them a witch doctor, I call them old people with good experience of family medicine and who give good assistance if somebody ill.

This person has gained knowledge concerning plants and bushes and so on by age and experience. The charge he or she make is a little donation; they might ask about two and six (12½p) which, in those days, was still a bit like £5! But if you have no money now, these people would let you pay little by little. If you didn't pay, then in future you get no help. In place like Mountainside it not like here with building knocked down and people move about country all time. We born in a place and we live in that place, that the way it used to be. If you spill milk, everybody know it, and they never forget. People is branded with how they are, they keep promise. If you did not pay debt, or if you wrong somebody, then you wear black cap and you never shake black cap off. It different here, and maybe it different in Jamaica now.

So for expert assistance it cost a bit, it only in drastic cases that you go to person with wisdom and long experience. I think these people save many lives. I tell you that this person, who do help for a bit of money, they also give assistance with animal, we had no veterinary surgeon and no money to pay if we had one.

But, I tell the truth, when it come to leaving the West Indies and coming to this country, I find it very hard to make up my mind. I have this friend, and she say that if it the last thing she ever do, it will be to come here. I tell her, maybe it not so easy in the Mother Country. I say, why change one farthing country for another. But she had already a mind made up.

I was betwist and between. Then somebody, a Jamaican man, show me some picture of England. These were not nice picture, I remember that these two eyes of mine saw a man rooting about in a dustbin! He slip what he find in his mouth. This really scared me. In Jamaica there was never need for hunger, nobody eat out of the trash can. This was the one bad thing I discover about the Mother Country, and my life in Jamaica was not like life in Heaven. You might think, 'Summer all year, that very nice!' But there were bad things, drastic things that I don't like to remember.

Once, as a young man, I left my father home, looking for work. I go right across Jamaica to Westmoreland, which is near Montego Bay. There was a bloody cane field there and it was terrible way of living. They have a barrack that used for maybe three hundred labourers. Three hundred sleeping in one big, long shed. I went and I ask for a job, any kind of work I will do. And the job I get is to hold the bull head.

You know when they cut cane, it be loaded on a cart pulled by what we call a bull-cow, an oxen maybe. There was boys, young men, to hold the head of this animal. This job is called holding bull head, or maybe running bull head. At no time is those bull supposed to walk. They must run all the time, and I have to run in front of them. And that isn't just two mile of running. It is running all day.

But a lot of young men want to run bull head. I was lucky to get that job, it pay a better wage. Holding bull head pay better because it is dangerous. Safest place is behind the bull, not running in front of him. The bull have two rope attached to his horn. One go to a man who sit on top of a pile of sugar cane, he has a whip and all the time he is whipping the bull, keep him moving fast. Everybody paid by the tonne. The other rope held by boy who run bull head. He run in front of the bull horns, and the bull run in front of the man who whip him.

Man, if I tell you my life, our life, in the West Indies... I do not want to even remember it sometime you know. I sit down and listen to some bloke talk, and it make me want to be sick. Mostly all who come here have been through same kind of life I been through.

That bloody cane field were over a hundred mile from Mountainside. I left my home to try get a bit of money for help at home where I have younger brothers and sisters. I was glad of that job leading the bull head. It make me bitter now that this could happen. It make me bitter that once I glad to get job running bull head. No man or woman, black, white, or any colour should have to do work in condition of that cane piece.

Man on the top drive the bull with his whip, and I running at the front, running and running all day in front of the bull, backwards and forwards, from field to scale, from scale to field. Running, running, running. I become tired. Maybe the bull become tired. These animal are nice animal, they tame, good bulls, but all the time they are driven and whipped, and the pressure show.

When a man pressure cow or bull, or anything, or anyone, something going to happen. I remember this, going to the scale, a certain amount of cane on the wagon, the bull pulling, under pressure, me running in front of the horn, under pressure. And man on top, and he is like wealthy people who run this country and all other country. He was on top like a rich man, driving, pushing the bull, and the bull, with two long, sharp horn, was pushing me. What happen next is that the bull get ignorant - I wasn't running fast enough for the bull, who getting a lot of whip.

I feel the horn coming down on me. Next it lift me up. This is the first time in my life I get really frighten, and it the first time I really know that life is Hell to survive. I feel the horn between my legs, I try to get forward off the horn, but the bull flash his head and pitch me some yards.

It's a lucky thing I weren't born to die in the West Indies. It's a lucky thing that he flash his head to the side, if he flash it forward, I wouldn't be living now. But he fling me yards to the side, right away from the wagon. I fall and the wagon run on a long way before the misterman on top can stop and come back to see if I alive or dead.

73

That is when I had my first really bitter feeling about rich, well off people who having it nice. And many Jamaican people have this feeling, they hate the bloody rich people, they hate the bloody rich white people and the red-face come-betweeners who dare only travel about with bodyguard or big dogs. And that day when the bull pitch me, I pray to God to get away from that terrible cane estate.

Now I live here, I don't say England is a land of milk and honey. I was told it was, but I don't find the milk and there was no honey for me here, but at least when I wanted work I get work. I work hard and I get a bit of money, and I take care of it. I have nothing bad to say about England, compared to that estate in Westmoreland. I don't even know how to tell you, who haven't known that place with its barrack, what it was like. A man wouldn't like his dog sit in that barrack for two hour, but we young men, we have to live there for some months. And don't think it was only young men. Young women live in that place as well, because young women need money, and they have to get money in that place... which ever way it take.

FOUR

MOTHER COUNTRY

I were over thirty and more or less settle: working cane piece, working my own rice field, a few animal, a bicycle, and so on. It were only by then I had enough money save to get to Mother Country. I think about it a lot. I wasn't doing bad anymore. I did start off doing bad, but I make change and make change, and I getting somewhere. So I didn't really feel happy about leaving. I ask a friend who has been to England for a short while: 'Why everybody so interested in going to England?' And he tell me just what everybody say: 'It the Mother Country where milk and honey flow'. I think to myself, it must be good if milk and honey flow there. Another thing he says is how cold it is in England. He say that in England it is necessary always to wear two pair of socks. Two pair!

So everybody is saying Go! Go! Go! and the film van is coming round and saying Go! Go! Go!

I don't believe everything I am told about Mother Country, but, in the end, I decide it best that I just go and see for myself. It were a big thing to do, to pack up and leave the country where I born, to leave the people I know, and to leave the woman I live with and our two children. But they would follow when I become establish in this land of milk and honey, and then we would be away from Jamaica where we had know so much Hell.

I'm not going to hide the truth as I know it. When we came to England, it were Hell here. Coloured always get the worse. Some days I am blasted bitter about life. When I think of some of the things life given out to me, here and in Jamaica, all I can do is tell what happen so that somebody might understand. Life is good and life is Hell and it the same life. Sometime you chose how you see it, sometime there no choice.

Running bull head is bad, now I tell you about another kind of bad. I'm in Leeds, working, not such a good job, but working, saving a bit of what I earn. Man come to Leeds from Ashton under Lyme, say there is plenty of work there, good work. So I get myself to Ashton, and I get this work in the factory. But can I get somewhere to live? No I cannot. It seem I the wrong colour for Ashton!

I tell you, I walk up every house door in that town, half the time they look through window and see it a coloured and don't even answer when I did knock. And them that answer, they say, 'Sorry, we have no room for you today.' And I know they have room. They have no room for me because I am coloured. I am black.

The day goes by and I walking and walking, knock this door, knock that door, walking, walking. I near wear out my boots. Every time I am turned away I feel a little bit smaller. In the end I no bigger than an insect... and I'm still knocking on them doors. But there was no room even for an insect because he was black.

So that is what happen to me in Ashton, looking for a place to lie my head and the people there make me feel like an insect. This no lie: by the end of day I even begin to think maybe it better if I do myself in. What I did do in the end was go back to the factory and find somewhere to sleep for the night there. They were working nightshift. I find a corner and curl up, I am very tired from all the walking.

Next I know somebody fetch the foreman and he wake me up. 'What you doing sleeping here, man?' he ask me. I tell him I got nowhere to sleep with a roof over my head. But he explain to me that I can't sleep in the factory either. 'If you sleep here,' he say, 'then soon all of you will want to sleep here. This is factory not lodging house.'

So I try again, looking for somewhere to hire a room that I might sleep indoors after my day work is through. But there is nowhere for a coloured man in Ashton, and, although I have a good job there, I have to pack it in and return to Leeds. That were in the nineteen sixties. Work here, work there, plenty of work in them days, but few English people want a coloured man sleeping under their roof.

I say this: it's bad if a neighbour isn't a neighbour because the skin colour doesn't suit. We might have disagreement about this and that, about politic or religion, sport or music, but what the devil have skin colour to do with it?

I don't know much now, but in those days I know

nothing. First thing I run into is that it take three week on a boat to get to this country. Nearly all my money is gone by the time I get to Southampton. And when I get here and look for somewhere to sleep, prior to finding my way around and beginning my new life here, I find that I must pay three week rent in advance. I am not used to such things. It all come as a big surprise to me. A friend who was working in this country told me he were earning £13 a week. That would be very good money in Jamaica, like a damned fool I had never ask what his living expenses were. Anyway, I travel by train to join him in the North of the country. I go to a place near Sheffield, where I understand I can get work with a company which make drainage pipes.

That first job were as hard as hell. But I wanted to get away from the pancrack, the Labour Exchange, so I take the first work I can get. You see, I make a few visit to Labour Exchange, but they had not anything to give me but hard times.

At that, call it a foundry, they set me on to work. I didn't know what wage I would earn, but the man say, 'Come on Monday morning, you can work here.' So on the Monday morning I went with my friend who also work there. I had to work a week in hand and by now I had little of my savings left - I had been travelling and looking for work for over a month. I was broke two weeks on, when I get my first wage packet in England. And with my first English wage packet I get another lesson to learn. I have to pay tax. I did not expect to pay tax on my first wage in England, because I have travelled a long way and kept myself, so that I can work in the Mother Country.

In my first wage packet, after two weeks work, with one week in hand, I find six pounds.

I'm telling you this: if there was a bridge across the sea long as from here to Hell, I would have walk it. But I had no fare to return, and there was no bridge, no road across the sea. So I realise that I must remain in Mother Country.

But what a country. It is difficult for me to explain to someone who is used to living here. In Mountainside I can shout to the man next door and he can't hear me. There was space. Things were clean. Southampton were a damned terrible sight to me.

For a long time I think England and I hear England and I talk England. When I get off the boat I was expecting to see something different from what I saw. There, then on the train coming to Yorkshire, I see nothing beside... well... call it a slum. Everywhere I look I see mucky, dirty buildings, and they all have chimneys. I didn't like all this dirt, but I think to myself, 'There must be plenty of work in this country with all these many factory.' Later I find out they were mostly just houses, but I did not know, we did not have houses like this in Jamaica.

I have to say this. I was shocked at the houses English people live in. The state of them, so mucky, I never seen a sight like this before. These buildings was looking very rough. At that time I did not know what caused this dirty, rough appearance, now I know it is smoke. But I say this as well, when I got to go in a few of these rough looking building I couldn't believe that the inside could be so great. All of them was lovely inside. But to look at the outside, you would say, 'I never like to go near these places.'

Looks are just outside appearance and don't tell you what inside is like - when you come from a country like Jamaica to one like England, you find that go for houses just like anything else.

I was in for a lot of shocks. And I keep thinking about that bridge and wishing it were built so I could walk back home. I find a place to live which is own by a Polish man. Early on I see him putting vegetable in a big pan. A very big pan. I ask how many he going to feed with all this vegetable. This is just his food. He make a week food in one pan.

Where is milk? Where is honey? Where is bridge? We might be poor at home, and not have many clothe, but we always have fresh food everyday, and plenty of it.

After some time at this foundry I decide that I had enough. Things must be better than this, so I start to look around for other work. Places like that is very hard for a worker, but it specially hard if you are a stranger. When you are a stranger you have to wait while you get used to things, then you might get the chance to move up to different grade. Truth is I was not getting enough to live on and I had two kids back in Jamaica to assist.

I was paying rent for a room that I share with three other single men. Four beds in a room that is only big enough for four bed and nothing else. The rent is thirty bob (£1.50), and around those times, this was a lot of money. I don't have much to spare!

At this time I really start to regret that I did scrap everything I have in Jamaica and come to this place. But there was no walking back, so I just had to stick it out. But bettering myself is a problem. I went to a mill where there was a job going. A gentleman there tells me I can start at the week end. I tell him I must work out my notice of one week, which I do. But when I go to the mill he just ask me what I there for. I say, 'I come for the job you give me.' And he say, 'There is no job. I forget about you and give the job to another man.'

So now I left with no job. I still have to pay rent and buy food, and I smoke as well. The little that I did save went very fast.

The job situation wasn't too bad then, but for coloured it were double bad. The most words I ever got in six week of seeking a job was: 'I'm sorry!… I'm sorry but there is no job!… No job!… Work is all gone!…' I was ashamed to hear those words. I still ashamed when I remember. I would see job in the paper at night, but when I approach, first thing in morning, it's always, 'I'm sorry, it gone!' And, you know, I doubt it was. I bloody doubt it was. I am coloured, I ashamed that in Mother Country I hear those words every day: 'Sorry, no jobs! Sorry jobs is all gone!'

Six week without work! It don't look long now. But then I had nothing, and it look to me long. I had no back-up, just me alone in this country, no mother or father, no brothers, no sister. And you go to the Labour Exchange: they push you around and swing you around and those days if you don't be careful it seem like you die for hungry before anything coming. I tell you, they wait to see you gasping before they offer a hand.

But after six week I get a letter from the railways at Huddersfield, where I am living. The letter say I can get work shunting. Well, no sooner have I the letter than I down at the station, and I get that job.

It was August time and I come to Leeds for training. Three weeks just learning the job, and they paying me to learn it!

Then I am working, dressed in provided uniform of black coat and trouser, carrying my long shunting pole. And I'm learning a lot. And very soon I learning what an English word mean. That word is winter!

In Jamaica there is no winter like in England. No fall or autumn, fruit go on growing, trees lose a few leaf, but you did not notice. It never get too cold; at Christmas, maybe you fasten a shirt button. But now I am in England I must learn what winter really mean.

It late October and I in my black jacket and long black coat. I have shunting pole under my arm and gloves on my hands and my hands in my pocket and, I tell you, I am nearby to freezing. Lucky we have a cabin with a fire where we can go to get warm every now and then.

I remember I go in the cabin, there are three English men there, keeping warm. I am shivering so much I can't speak. I just go and stand real close to that fire and shiver till I feel the warm coming through. Then there was a funny smell and the Englishmen laugh. I laugh with them. I am on fire. I was warm enough, but my coat back was burning! It was my first winter, I had a lot to learn.

I go back outside to the shunting and I saw something coming down, just falling slowly. White bits falling out of the sky. This is puzzling to me, I think to myself of how I heard about manna falling from heaven. But I did not think that this could be manna. I didn't know what it could be. I went back into the cabin and say to the English bloke, 'I seen something falling, what it is?' And the English bloke say to wait inside a while and I will see a lot more.

After a bit this stuff is white all over the floor and I go out to see it better and to taste it. It was water! I never seen anything like this in my life. I hear about snow, but I did never seen it and nobody did ever tell me what is the colour of snow. So that was snow: white and it taste just like an ordinary thing, like water. After a bit I am used to it and I think that is the end of the matter. We have had snowfall and soon it will go away. But it doesn't go away. Next morning it still there, but now it like rock on the floor and I slide and skid all the way to work. And it still blasted cold. Cold like I did not think it could be cold. And that day I have something else to learn about cold.

Where I went wrong that next day of snow was wanting to go to lavatory. I went to lavatory, but it so cold that day I couldn't find no way to pull my buttons open. So now I learning the hard way. I just stand there and no matter how I try I can't pull my buttons undone! I wont go no further with this, I just leave it to you.

After that day, whenever it freezing...I leave me front door open! You have to live and learn.

So I wasn't doing bad now, and I was still saving a little bit each week. After a bit I decide that I did not want to live all my life in a single room that I share with others and pay a rent for. There was a house I see in Huddersfield, it were very dilapidated condition, but it were for sale. I bought it for £350: two room down, two room up, and an attic. I get a lot of help from my friends, we work very hard on that house and make it into a decent place to live in, which it had not been when it were for sale.

Soon that house was full. That house did well for me because in those days there were no English people would rent a foreigner a room, especially if he were coloured man. Only the Poles in Huddersfield would rent room to a coloured man and we would say that some of them was near enough criminal. If you rented a room you had gas meter and electric meter and you find you had to give a lot of money, a lot of money on top of the rent you must pay.

So it was not long in that house, after it all done up and decorated, that I have more people than I want sharing it with me. I bought the house but soon it paid for itself. From there, about 1969, my luck changed. From I bought that dilapidated house in Huddersfield things start to change for the better. I married in Huddersfield. I bought another house in Huddersfield. Then I got fed up with Huddersfield and move to Leeds.

In Leeds I settle. The woman I live with in Jamaica never did come here. She always suffer from rheumatism and we think that this cold country would harm her. My kids there is grown up now. I left the railway and tried my hand at other things. In the end I worked for ten years at a soft drink firm. I work night and I the only coloured there. I work hard, turn my hand to whatever is needed. When I retired, they give me a present, and a pension.

I tell you this, you might say I have had a hard life, and I have had a hard life in England and in Jamaica, but I won't talk about all the hard times. If I put in all the hard times coloured people going to see it and say, 'Bloody hell, that man who write this is trying to be lowering the country.' Some men try to be big when they not, well, I'm not one of them. I never say that I am coming from Heaven to this country, or that I rich in Jamaica. Why should I tell lies? In Jamaica when I there we had no Labour Exchange, no DHSS, for help there was only friends and family. At Christmas, when the band play and move from house to house, everybody is friend, but rest of year round, people look after their own business.

Even the poor ones, even the old ones, they have no pension like they have pension here, they never get more than a shilling a week. And to get one shilling a week they must see the Pauper Agent. If they really in bad way, Pauper Agent might allow one shilling and sixpence. I believe Government say our old people should get more than that, maybe five shilling, maybe even ten. I don't know how much. Nobody in Mountainside know how much, not when I were there. All we know was that Pauper Agent were another come-betweener, like red-face, like pan-head. Pauper Agent were a coloured, like us, but he get a bit of education and he use it to get a bit of money. We think some of that money he get were on it way to our old people. But there is no television to tell these things. And if somebody with a little education complain... he soon become Pauper Agent Assistant and help pay the shilling a week. In Jamaica, as I know it, every man have a price, he can be bought. I ask you. Who can afford to buy? Did poor man ever buy rich man? Every body could be bought, from judges down, but the poor could never do any of this buying. Is this a fair country?

Some people would say West Indies was well off. It was bad. Most of our country was run by England, which we taught to call Mother Country. And I do believe what I told, that England assisted West Indies with many thousand or even million of pounds every year. But, you know, somebody dip there hand in it even before it leave this country. That's what I think. And when that money do reach Jamaica... it was like ants and sugar! You know how much bits of sugar the ants will shift? I know this, when that money get down to the poor people of Jamaica, there was nothing left. The ants had it all.

So we born poor and we live poor. I left Jamaica poor, and I am still poor. But I think to myself, if I was back in the West Indies, I wouldn't be better off than I am now. And I've seen other countries. These days America very big. People from Jamaica visit America and they pick fruit and, I am told, earn good money. But I have been to America and I have no longing to return.

I went to New Jersey, to see my cousin who I had not seen for many years, since he left Spanish Town. It were a lot different from England. Americans race cars in the street, the street were so broad. I were only there for a week, but, you know, in all that week I never hardly see two people walking, they all drive in car. Long straight streets, maybe two mile of straight street. I think to myself, I wanted a ring, something as a souvenir to remember this place by. I tell my friends this, and they say they will show me where I might buy a ring. There were three of us and we take a cab, or taxi as it called here, then we leave the cab and walk down a street of shops. Now these men I with are coloured and they know that we shouldn't be going down this street. I knew nothing of streets in America, of the ways of America, I there for one week only, I was having a holiday! I think my cousin thought that being I from England he'd just let me go along and see what happen. I believe that these friends of mine think that because I am from England now it could be all right for us to be in this part of the town. We might be lucky. They was pinning their hope on me.

Well, as we go down this street in New Jersey, all I see is guns and gun shop all over. I didn't want no gun, I wanted a ring.

In the end we find a shop which sell rings and go in. Straight away I see a lovely ring, under the glass of the counter. This ring has three diamonds which look like eyes. So I am looking a lot at this ring, through the glass, but, before I had a chance to ask, 'How much this ring is?' I see two policeman standing behind me. They say, 'What you doing in here? What you all doing in here?' The bloke I am with just look at the police, but provide no answer. Then the police them say, 'Come on! What you doing in here?' and I say, 'Why?' And they say, 'Don't you know you shouldn't be in here? You shouldn't be down this street. Where you from?' I say England, and I tell him I want to buy ring as present to take back from holiday. Then him say, 'Look, you don't come down this street! You don't come in this store! I give you a chance, and I give them a chance, because you from England and you don't know the rules of America.' And he tell us get out of that store and leave that part of town and not return.

I tell you, I don't want to go on street like that again. There was no coloured in that area. I start to think, England is a lot different from America. In England, so long as you behave yourself, you can go where you want. America, was different, they kick you out of some area no matter how you behave. In that part of America where my cousin live they was operating a colour bar, a real colour bar like I never come across in England. Here there are pubs were you not made welcome, but it is not formal, and the police don't operate the colour bar in the way they did in New Jersey.

So things are not perfect in America. It a rich country, but there are plenty of poor there, and many people must live in the street, and some are hungry. But here in England I find few faults that I could easily change. And rough as it is now, when old people die cold, Government of this country make sure nobody die with hunger. And that is Government, not ordinary English people as I come to know them..

As to English people, I find them friendly most of time. I live with English neighbours and I have not time for coloured who say 'English people this... English people that...' We all people, good and bad. When I come here I know nothing. If I go into Woolworth I did not know how to get out. I lost every day, every where. Who you think help me to find way? Who help me to settle in this country? English people, white people. So I say, judge by how people are with you, not by what colour of skin or how they talk is sounding.

It is rough now, and it getting rougher. People say Margaret Thatcher! Margaret Thatcher! They blame this woman for everything. And I know that many time she is like President Reagan, who is man who throw stone then hide his hand. And I know people peep through key hole and tell how the stone thrower hand is moving. And I have little tolerance for Margaret Thatcher who is all out for herself and her group of people. But tell me, who going to step in Margaret Thatcher shoes and not grab it all for themselves and their group? Do you think Kinnock or Owen going into 10 Downing Street and we going to find ourself in feather bed? It take a lot of waiting before that happen!

People going to have to work like Hell, and this country going to have to do the same. There are problem here, big problem, but if I think back to how my father had to live... he had it harder. There were big blokes around then who made sure that not much came down to the poor, things like that don't change much. And now things are getting worse in this country. It wasn't all good before Thatcher, but now there is little good at all. Before her the Unions they had a bit of power, they could talk, they could help. Now, if you go outside and say, 'I'm in Union!' it come out as if you saying, 'I'm in dustbin!'.

Thatcher and her people do that and there is nothing I can do, or you can do, unless we get together. And I believe we must get together. If there are many more years of this kind of government, she'll wipe Union that flat that there will be no Union. And I tell you I have seen the disadvantage to people where there is no Union.

As a young man I have seen boss ride round on his horse, ride round the cane piece. If that man see somebody who not working fast he did take a whip to him. A horse whip. My eyes have seen this. No man should have horse whip on him, whatever colour. Now when the Union form in Jamaica, the boss stop whipping and the worker get a little bit of strength. If the boss go too far there is strike, maybe the cane field and sheds is fired. We stand together because together we have strength.

If Union is broke in England, then you will come to know what is Hell, like my father know, and like I know when I was still a young man. And there is other whip beside one that fall on back, there is whip for stomach and for head and for heart. I see all these whip as young man, I pray to God I never see them again.

FIVE

WHAT REALLY HAPPEN IN THE GARDEN

I come close to end of my story now. But there still a few things I want to tell. A few year back, I buy this house were I live now. I always hope that I would get a house with a piece of land so that I might grow things, like I had done in Jamaica. This were my first chance of having a little garden. Now I am to find that what I have grow in Jamaica I can't grow here. And many of the plant that grow here I never see in Jamaica. In the West Indies we grow potato, but not like you grow here. And we don't have garden, we have field, maybe two three acre for an ordinary man. If you have five six, maybe eight people in one house, you need a good size field to feed all the people in that house. You see I am used to providing food for a family from a field.

After I leave work, to retire, I decide I need something to occupy my time. A friend of mine say to get plot. Well I didn't know what is plot. Anyway, we go take a look at plot. When I see it, I were kind of stuck. The other people with plot, or allotment, grow all sort of thing, but I been in the country all this time and I never did plant anything before garden, where I grow just a few root of flower and vegetable.

Anyway, friend help me get plot. At beginning I get advice from no one, I just use what I know from when

I were cultivating in the West Indies. When I start on the garden I just dig it and plant it, dig and plant. But when I start on this plot business I were still daft. I didn't know the English way of planting. In the West Indies when you say you are going to plant something, you plant just how you like. We don't have plot, we have field, you can plant how you like and have land left over. This plot, this allotment, seem like some kind of economy field: you have to grow plants all crush together, no space for spread out and breath.

First year I got that plot I were late. I plant some potato and a few cabbage. Being late I didn't see much progress, but still, it was better than doing nothing. And as I go along, I start to pick up. I start to find myself doing things like the rest of the English and Irish that have plots about mine.

Being retire I spend a lot of time tending my plot. Everyday in the summer I give all my plants a good wetting, I think that why my plants are so big and pretty when they grow. And I experiment with my plants. First year I grow beans I put lime on the land for some of them, no lime for the other. I find that the ones that grow on the lime land is much bigger, fatter: so this way I have learn something about cultivation in England.

I don't like chemical on my land. The plant is going to be made out of the land, and my son is going to be made out of the plant, so I don't want my little boy to be made out of these chemical fertiliser. I grow my plants only in a natural way. I dig in to the soil a lot of horse muck, and that the only fertiliser I ever use, apart from lime, which I think is good for the soil. These are natural things, so I grow natural plants which harm nobody.

In summer I sometimes tend my plot from five o'clock in the morning until the same time at night. And maybe later on I walk up for another look to make sure there's been no vandalism.

This plot is about a quarter of a mile from my house. I have a small green-house there, and water can be drawn from a tap which is nearby. I grow many English plant: enough potato and onion to feed my family through the winter. And I freeze broad bean, cauliflower and sweet corn. My son love sweet corn so I grow quite a few root of it.

I'd like to be self-sufficient in everything. I grow grape vine in my greenhouse now, but not enough to make wine for all year round. But I do grow a little tobacco. This year I have grown two kind of tobacco, and I have treat the dried leaves with whisky, molasses, honey, and a little vinegar. Experimenting again to find the nicest smoke. I give some to my friend, and some to my wife for making cigarette, and I have some left over to enjoy in my pipe.

One problem you have with plot is damned kids. If I don't spend a lot of time at plot when the plants are big and pretty, kids come and pull them up, or they break into my green house, smashing panes of glass, try and steal the grapes. And it not only kids. Last year, just before I harvest my potato, somebody come and dig up a couple of sack-fulls for theyselves.

It make me bloody angry, all that money for manure and seed potato, then all the digging and planting and wetting, and some bugger just steal them.

In my garden now I grow just a few root of lettuce and cabbage. Mainly in my garden and yard I grow flowers, Dahlia I like a lot. And I have apple tree that bear very well, pretty red apple. I like my garden, but like all garden it has snakes, by which I mean there are local kids who steal the apple. I talk with my neighbour and we say what we do to these kids if we catch them. Then we talk about the way we behave concerning stealing fruit when we were kids, then we laugh and the loss of our apple is not such a great disaster.

Well, we had it rough in some ways, today kids have it rough in others.

I don't complain about time I spend at plot, I take a flask of tea, and have my pipe which I sometimes smoke, sitting on a chair which I keep in the greenhouse. For a while I had a bottle of my own wine which I hide at the plot: damned kids find that and pour it over the tomato plant!

I still glad that I did get that plot. It something to do. It help to keep me away from bookie, it help to keep me away from pub, and it help to keep me away from trouble.

If you've no work and nothing to do, it a right miserable state to be in. Gardening or cultivating is very hard work if you do it properly. I have a plot and a half, which is all I can manage. I work plot damn hard. When I not digging or weeding or wetting I spend lot of time observing my plant, thinking about how it doing, what to do next. In winter, which I do not like, when there is snow and ice, I am jumpy, waiting for when I can work again. Cut it short: plot give me great satisfaction and it save me money.

So maybe you say, here is happy man. I have house and garden, I have wife and little boy, and I have a plot which give me much hard work and satisfaction. I didn't have it easy in my life, maybe that is why I am contented now. And I am contented now, but not in every way. When I sit in my greenhouse with flask of tea and pipe, I sometime smiling because plant are growing well, but sometime I thinking about other things that do not make me smile.

All my life I work hard, sometime two job. When I get home I must sleep, or maybe I go to pub and try to forget work, try to forget how I treat for being coloured, try and find little enjoyment. Up to now I don't do much thinking about life, about where I come from and where I going. Now I retire from paid work, I doing a lot of thinking, sorting thing out in my head. I tell you, sometime I sit in greenhouse and I sick with anger.

These things are difficult to say in words, complicated as Hell. Maybe some people will read what I put and think, This man is very ignorant or simple - but I have thought about these things a great deal, and I do not find them simple. And is not ignorance to ask question and seek answer.

When I was child I was treat as child. I was told many lies, like all children are told lies. These lies are told to make children behave good. For instance, when I small, and the wind whistle and howl round the house where I live, and I tremble in my shirt for fear, Mother used to say: 'Slave Master coming! You be good boy or Slave Master take you!' It were not true, noise was the wind whistling and my mother tell me lie to control me. Children don't know much and for this reason they can be control by untrue stories.

At school, when I did go to school, teacher tell stories from Bible. Only stories ever told to me as a kid were from Bible. My mother don't tell me stories, and my father work so hard I don't see him long enough for stories. Father ask me if I done my work with the animals; is everything fine concerning cultivation of field?

With my eyes and my hands I learn about things around me, how to control horse or catch wild animal or grow plant. With my ears I learn stories told by teacher: God make Adam first man and give he Eve and they live together in Garden of Eden. Then come snake and Eve have son call Cain, then come son call Abel who a kind and gentle person. According to his Dad way of thinking, Cain were a funny bloke, in the end he kill brother Abel. Then Cain sent to another place to find woman and make more children.

As a kid I believe this, I told to believe, I made to believe. As I get older I start to ask question: Who is woman Cain find? Where she from? When I have the chance, with educated people, I keep on asking question: Cain and Abel, do they have the same father? Where did this Eve drop from? Out of sky! What is snake all about? Jonah and the whale: how I to know that whale isn't olden day name for submarine?

I did try to answer these question. I try damn hard, for instance, I think, maybe Cain did not even find woman, maybe he find an animal, a monkey. Maybe he find a white animal, maybe he find a black animal. In the end I think, Why should I believe anything I told as a child. If I don't see and touch it, why should I believe it? They told me enough lies and kid stories, maybe it all lies.

And these lies are still told, and they are not lies for educated people. These are the lies powerful people tell poor people. People tell me lies when I a boy, and they still telling me kid lies when I am man. I angry to be treat like a child. But that is nothing! It is when I think why these lies told that I am near being sick with anger.

It seem to me that such children stories and lies are told to keep rich people rich and poor people poor, to keep weak people weak and powerful people powerful. It seem to me that I were told to believe such things so that I would be good boy all my life. And good boy work like hell all his life. And it did not matter how hard that good boy work because the rich stay rich and the poor stay poor.

When I were young boy, I go to see Great Grandmother and she have little house and little plot of land. Grandfather work hard all his life, Father work hard all his life, I work hard all my life. And what have

I got? I got the same as Great Grandmother Mary: little house and little plot of land.

So I come back to stories, and now I believe this: all my life I have been told lies fit only for children, and these lies were told to keep me and people like me under control.

I am told that God give Moses the Ten Commandments, that He write them in rock with a pen of fire. I never saw pen of fire, but I know Commandments; they burnt into me at school. I have thought about Commandments all my life. In Spanish Town I lose my first shirt, which I love, in order to see film of Commandments. Now I believe they are not written by God, they are written by the rich and powerful and they written to control the poor and weak. Just like when Mother say: Slave Master coming

Thou shalt not steal - who can the poor steal from if not the rich? Thou shalt not murder? Who the poor going to murder? And for what reason? Thou shalt not covet that which is owned by your neighbour... what the poor neighbour have that can be coveted? I tell you, when I hear these word, and when I hear about Adam and Eve and Garden of Eden, I think: 'Be good boy or Slave Master take you', and I sick with anger that grown people all over world are controlled by lies and kids story.

All poor people, every colour, everywhere, is underneath same whip, and it the whip of wealth and power. The lies told to uneducated people, to poor people. Lies like a rein and bit to steer us, go this way, go that way, stop, start. Who do you think is doing the steering? I tell you: it the rich. And I tell you something else, such people don't believe the stories, and they don't think much about what the Bible say. Love thy neighbour? The rich ones love only their riches, their position and their power!

Do not misunderstand me. I believe that everybody have gods, some people make god out of motor car or gold ring. I don't believe in god like that.. a thing. I think there is God, supreme God. I can't see this God, but I sometime feel I might almost hear this God. I don't understand what is this God. I don't understand why this God allow children to starve and be killed. So God I believe is invisible and difficult to understand, but I do believe, because sometime I can feel this God.

So mistake I make early in life is not in God. Mistake I make is to believe in religion. Now, after much thinking, I understand religion: it just Slave Master, whistling and howling in the trees. If I had know that fifty year ago, my life might have been a bit different.

SEASIDE

Mountainside was not too close to the sea, and the first time I saw the sea was when I start to roam. You know how boys of thirteen try to roam. And one day me and my mate we walk for maybe two hour... and we find the sea.

The sea soon become a place we try to get to, you know why? It because of the women you find there. These women are standing and seated round a big fire and they hanging fish on a long string. The reason for this is that they are cooking fish. As boys we was always interested in food.

Also we see fisherman is there, when he bring in the boat, onto the sand, we run by the side of the boat, trying to look in, see what he catch. Him say, Go to hell! What you want? We say, Beg a fish, Sir! And he pick put four or five fishes and throw them on the sand. These fish is mostly small ones, but they was great to us. When we get this fish, we go by the women fire, so soon as they roast they fish and move away for a little time we always there, waiting to roast fish we got. No matter what kind fish the man give us, when we roast them they taste right nice. And sometime we can get so many fish like this that we take some home.

**Alfred Williams and Ray Brown,
Leeds, 1987.**

ALFRED DIED IN WHEATFIELDS HOSPICE, LEEDS. 16TH APRIL 1997.

Tribute to Alfred, Yorkshire Artscene, May 1997

ALFRED WILLIAMS 1917 - 1997.

I met Alfred Williams in 1980. A Jamaican, dignified in battered, wide-brimmed brown trilby and British Rail donkey jacket. He introduced himself as George.

In 1987 we wrote his life story: TO LIVE IT IS TO KNOW IT. When Yorkshire Art Circus had the manuscript, I asked him how he would like his name - and he sprang *Alfred* on me. His given name, given by his mother and granny. 'George', after Chicken George, in ROOTS, was also a given name, given by the workers at Canada Dry, when Alfred joined them: the first black man!

Writing with Alfred was wonderful. His words were considered, tested against experience and a deep understanding that derived from the flow of his broad, intricate and intensely lived days. He'd seen men horse-whipped; his shoulders carried scars from burdens so heavy they broke his skin.

Six days before he died, of multiple cancers, he asked if I thought he would recover. I said no. He said, 'That what I been thinking, man.' Two days later he told me he'd decided to go. Like so many, the statement was metaphorical: '...no time to do up house, man... too many repair needed...' He asked if I understood. I said I did. He thanked me.

Next day he was taken into hospital. He died with dignity forty eight hours later.

His family and my partner, Rose (Lady Bird to Alfred), ensured he was never alone. We held his hand, smiled, maintained eye-contact.

His body was skeletal. Arms once tight with muscle and shiny with health (he carried big bags of potatoes and leeks to our '96 bonfire party) became wrinkled, lustreless skin sagging from bone and tendon. His eyes became mysterious.

The last night I handed over to his son, Michael, a tough eighteen year old who cradled Alfred's head and stroked the tightly curled white hair. Alfred summoned up a voice from deep in his chest. 'Take care, man. I'll see you.'

He survived the night. I returned with slicked hair and shocking pink shirt and tie. His eyes took me in slowly. His mouth, now flaccid and almost lifeless, twitched at one corner. He gave a slow nod. And that was our last communication.

He lives on in TO LIVE IT IS TO KNOW IT. And he's in me until my house tumbles.

Eulogy for Alfred, delivered at his funeral in the Seventh Day Adventists Church, Meanwood Road, Leeds. Friday 25ᵗʰ April, 1997.

I met Alfred Williams sixteen years ago, when Rose and I became his neighbours in Kirkstall.

Soon after we arrived, he retired from Canada Dry. With the strength and enthusiasm of someone half his age, he took to cultivating. Alfred's plot, which came to mean so much to him, was a double allotment, by the railway line. To it he brought his experience of farming in Jamaica, advice from all quarters, and careful observation of other gardeners... he mixed it all together... then did what felt right. The results were wonderful: sweet corn, cabbage, grapes, and peppers... coriander, kalaloo, and massive orange pumpkins.

He grew strong, perfect plants. He always used the same expression: big and pretty. Big and pretty flowers, big and pretty leeks, big and pretty onions...

We all have good memories of this man. I think of nights round our kitchen table, when Alfred, Rose, and I shared our happiness, our problems, our sorrows, our dreams, but most of all our laughter.

His judgement was based on wisdom and experience. If he said, 'I don't agree with you, but I understand why you doing it' - I was content. If he said, 'That's what I'd do, man' - I was happy.

Ten years ago we wrote his biography - TO LIVE IT IS TO KNOW IT. Many people learned a lot from Alfred's life story.

For me, working with him was a privilege... Knowing him a joy.

He was a big and pretty man, full of dignity, courage, and humour.

His life was a struggle... He knew that that was how life should be.

No one can replace him... Alfred was special.